peppers peppers peppers peppers

peppers peppers peppers

Marlena Spieler

FIREFLY BOOKS

A FIREFLY BOOK

Published by Firefly Books Ltd. 1999

First Printing

Library of Congress Cataloguing
in Publication Data is available.

Canadian Cataloguing in Publication Data
Spieler, Marlena
Peppers, peppers, peppers: jalapeño, chipotle, serrano, sweet bell,
poblano and more—in a riot of color and flavor

Includes index.
ISBN 1-55209-319-0

1. Cookery (Peppers). 2. Peppers. I. Title.
TX803.P46S64 1999 641.6'384 C98-932464-8

Published in Canada in 1999 by
Firefly Books Ltd.
3680 Victoria Park Avenue
Willowdale, Ontario
M2H 3K1

Published in the United States in 1999 by
Firefly Books (U.S.) Inc.
P.O. Box 1338, Ellicott Station
Buffalo, New York
14205

This book was designed and produced by
Quintet Publishing Limited
6 Blundell Street London N7 9BH

Creative Director: Richard Dewing
Art Director: Silke Braun
Design: Squid Inc.
Senior Editor: Clare Hubbard
Editor: Anna Bennett
Illustrator: Jane Smith

Typeset in Great Britain by
Central Southern Typesetters, Eastbourne

Manufactured in Malaysia by CH Colour Scan Sdn. Bhd.

Printed in China by Leefung-Asco Printers Ltd.

Picture Credits
GNS Spices Inc: pp 12, 22; Life File: pp 11 (t), 14 (b);
Peter Newark's American Pictures: pp 10 (t), 25 (t);
Sea Spring Photos: pp 10 (b), 13, 14 (t), 15 (t);
Peter Wilson: pp 11 (b), 17 (b).

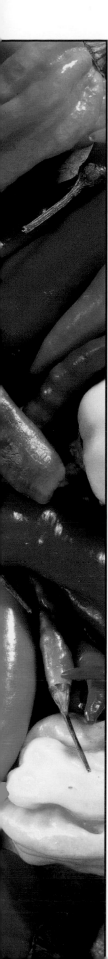

Contents

Acknowledgments

Thanks are due to the following: Clare Hubbard, my editor, for asking me to write this book. My agent Borra Garson; my husband Alan who has filled our apartment with peppers (and we have a big apartment). Leah Spieler, of whom I am inordinately proud. Jon Harford, for a myriad of special things, especially helping me to find my way in cyberspace. Gretchen Spieler for taking us to Cuban Sandwiches. Grandmother "Bachi" Sophia Dubowsky, for kindling my interest in peppers, indeed in all things edible.

The San Francisco Chronicle for commissioning me to write one fascinating article after another, year after year: Michael Bauer, M.A. Mariner, Miriam Morgan, Fran Irwin; and to Ethel Brennan for making it all look beautiful. To Colman Andrews at *Saveur* magazine for commissioning an article on falafel in Israel, which enriched my pepper and chile repertoire enormously. Michael Bateman of the *Independent on Sunday* for his wealth of information and enthusiasm for all peppers.

Dodie Miller, and her Cool Chilli Co. for making the wide variety of dried chiles available to us in Britain. Michael and Joy Michaud for growing fresh chiles in Britain and selling them via mail order (Peppers by Post).

The Greenery for sharing with me a wealth of fine peppers: red, yellow, green, purple, fat, long, tiny, and huge; Countrywide Porter Novelli Limited for their pepper varieties and information. Jim Heppel, Chief Executive and Mike Culverwell, Superintendent for the Corporation of London, New Spitalfields Market took me by the hand and led me through the wonderland of New Spitalfields Market. David Reynolds of Reynolds Catering Supplies Ltd at the Market, who sent me spectacular samples of his peppers. Debra Pieri of the Fresh Fruit and Vegetable Information Bureau offered expertise. Epicure Foods for their delicious sun-dried peppers.

Friends in tasting: Paula Eve Aspin, who likes it hot. Richard Hudd who can find the wine to go with it. Dr. Esther Novak and Rev. John Chendo; Alexa Stace, a friend in stirring. Sue Kreitzman, herself as bright as a pepper. Sri and Roger Owen for Gado Gado and Indonesian duck and general life inspiration. Kamala Friedman, an inspiration in pickling, and Tim Hemmeter and Amanda Hamilton, true originals. Sandy Wax; Etty, Bruce and Natalie Blackman; Paul Richardson; Pierre Parini. Fred and Mary Barclay; Jerome Freeman and Sheila Hannon who taught me to never be afraid of a soufflé; Nigel Patrick and Graham Ketteringham.

Lynette and Kaeomy McLaughlan who like peppers, even hot ones. Opper cousins Melissa and Stephen who are good little cooks and connoisseurs; Alison, Sparky, and Lexie; Jordan. Auntie Estelle and Uncle Sy Opper.

To my parents: Caroline and Izzy Smith who like peppers, and pickles even better. And last of all, to Freud, never an ordinary moggy: we miss you.

about the pepper

Ever since Christopher Columbus introduced the pepper into European cuisine the popularity of all types of edible pepper has grown throughout the world. This chapter details their fascinating history as well as the practicalities of preparing and cooking them.

introduction

When I was a child in California, the peppers in our local markets were green, mostly, except in the fall when they ripened to a scarlet hue and tasted as sweet as dessert. We ate them whole, biting into them as if they were apples (a habit I still retain).

Later, as I learned to cook, I discovered that these juicy red fruits were the same as the silky red peppers I had enjoyed pickled and roasted in jars, and related to the smoky red strips of pimiento I plucked out of briny green olives whenever I had the chance. California's Mexican heritage meant that, of course, I grew up eating hot peppers and chiles. Mexican cuisines are based on a wide variety of chiles, from mild and sweet to breathtakingly hot, and Californian cuisine evolved around those flavors, with strong Latin American, Mediterranean, and Pacific Rim influences.

At home, relatives and family friends made Eastern European dishes of roasted peppers with eggplant, simmered peppers and paprika, or braised meats with onions and peppers. New York's Little Italy meant meatball and pepper sandwiches, pepper frittatas, and a Mediterranean flavor which I have loved ever since.

Moving to Israel opened my eyes to even more peppery flavors, and by the time I grew up, I knew my path through life would probably be accompanied by peppers, chiles, and the cuisines from which they originate.

pepper anatomy

Peppers grow in abundance throughout the world's warm climates, having originated hundreds of years ago in South and Latin America. There are four basic types of chiles: *Capsicum annuum*, which probably originated in Mexico, *Capsicum Baccatum*, from Argentina and much of South America, *Capsicum frutescens*, from Panama, and *Capsicum chinense* from the Amazon Basin via the Caribbean.

After their introduction to the Old World, chiles flourished in warm climates, spicing up Indian, Thai, Korean, Vietnamese, Indonesian, even African food. Previously, great quantities of black peppercorns had been used to make dishes fiery in taste. Although commonly known as "peppers," Capsicums are in no way related to peppercorns. Like tomatoes and eggplants, they are classed botanically as fruit vegetables.

This varied vegetable family is known botanically as Capsicum, the word derived from the Latin, *capsa*, (box), a term which refers to the fact that they "encapsulate" seeds inside them.

Capsicums come in a vast array — sweet, hot, large, small, dark green and sweet red, yellow, and orange ones, with a wide range of flavors and levels of heat. In South America there are tiny lilac chiles, in the Southwestern United States you will find brownish peppers, and in India pale green chiles that are dried to a white fiery powder.

More than 2,000 named chile varieties exist, with such a myriad of cross-pollinations that you need only to add zeros to this number. They cross-pollinate wherever they are planted, creating even more color, flavor, and heat permutations.

Nutritionally, the pepper is rich in goodness. One medium-sized pepper will provide almost the entire daily adult vitamin C requirement. Both green and red peppers are high in vitamin A, the red pepper ten times more than the green.

Peppers also contain vitamins such as B1, B2, and D, minerals such as calcium, phosphorus, and iron, plus fiber, pectin, and essential nutrients, all packaged into a mere 15 calories per 3$^{1}/_{2}$-oz/100-g.

About the Pepper

The fiery, berrylike little pepper which Christopher Columbus introduced to Europe on his return from his voyage to the New World eventually came to thrive in the soil of southern Europe. Later, Portuguese and Spanish explorers spread an even wider variety of chiles and peppers they had encountered on their voyages. Peppers and chiles have been eaten in the New World for more than 7,000 years—native cuisines such as the Aztec, Inca, and Zapotec are strongly based on them, and the basis for their reputedly magical powers originates with the Chavin culture in the Peruvian Andes, which erected a huge monolith as a paean to them. But the cuisines of the Far East, Australia, Africa, Europe, and the Mediterranean, which owe so much of their distinctive vigor and flavor to these vegetables, have only known the plant since 1493, a relatively short period of time.

Christopher Columbus landed in the New World on October 12, 1492, where he had his first taste of the chile pepper.

Soon Hungarian food was red with paprika (a hot form of ground chiles), Italian food was rich with peppers, Indian curries were scorched with chiles, and African food too was fired with hot peppers. The cuisines of the Old World were truly transformed, and have never looked back.

Fiercely hot, the Thai chile pepper is grown throughout Asia. Gives a tasty kick to stir-fries.

Although Indian cuisine is famed for its hot, spicy flavor, the chile pepper has only been known to that culture since the fifteenth century.

Cuisines Peppered with Peppers

Throughout the Mediterranean sweet peppers of all colors, round or sometimes long and pointed, are eaten with enjoyment. Specialties such as roasted peppers in salads, coulis, purées, and sauces for all sorts of pastas, meats, and fish are found from Provence to Italy, Greece, and Turkey, through the Near East, and across North Africa and up again through Spain. Hot peppers are also eaten in many of these areas, too.

Paprika is widely used in Eastern European dishes, together with a whole range of mild and spicy peppers cooked with the mushrooms, sauerkraut, potatoes, vegetables, and meats that make up their cuisines. Northern Europe has only recently discovered the many different colors of peppers but has taken to them in a big way, even if only in salads.

Throughout Asia, whether India, China, Japan, Korea, Vietnam, Thailand, Laos, Indonesia, or Pakistan, peppers are a staple: usually hot peppers, fresh, dried, and ground, chopped and stewed, made into chutneys and hot pickles.

The entire circle of the countries that touch the Pacific from America's West Coast, through the Far East, Australia, and New Zealand, and back up the coast of California, has yielded up a cross-cultural cuisine known as Pacific Rim, sparked by East-West flavors and traditions, with chiles and peppers at its heart.

African foods are often very hot, especially in Ethiopia where berebere, a mixture of chiles and spices, is used to flavor many dishes. Fresh chili paste, awaze, is another basic dish.

South and Central America is the chile's original home, and the foods there are often based on the pepper. In North America, too, both peppers and chiles have long been popular, especially in Mexico where the variety of shape, size, and flavor is endless. Peppers are even popular among groups where it is not a part of the culture.

Hot spicy chiles hanging up to dry in a bar in Budapest, Hungary. The chiles are ground and made into paprika.

the growth *of the pepper*

Sweet (bell) peppers are grown in the sunniest, mildest climates, whereas the hotter and most flavorful varieties seem to come from the hottest regions. Holland is a huge exporter both of sweet peppers and sometimes of chiles, growing them indoors in greenhouses for year-round availability. The Canary Islands, Spain, and Israel with their warmer climates also supply the European market all year round. Kenya grows a large amount of green chiles for export.

In North America most peppers and chiles come from California and Mexico. Central America boasts a large commercial chile-growing industry: Honduras, Colombia, Costa Rica, and Belize grow cayennes, tabasco peppers, and habaneros for sauces and relishes, with Guatemala, Panama, and Venezuela also growing chiles that are eaten all over the world. India and Pakistan as well as the countries of southeast Asia grow an abundance of chiles, exporting them as dried spices and prepared sauces.

While you might expect hot and spicy foods to be most popular where the weather is cold, the opposite is true. Hot peppers grow abundantly where the weather is hot and sultry, and stimulate the sweat glands, which is very important in hot climates. They also stimulate your taste buds and make you salivate, perking up your appetite.

The Red Savina™ Habanero pepper grown by GNS Spices Inc. in California, is recorded in The Guinness Book of World Records *as the world's hottest spice.*

A Red Savina™ production field.

Growing your own Peppers

All peppers, both hot and sweet, are native to South and Central America. These like warm climates, so to grow them in colder climates you must wait until after all danger of frost has passed before either sowing the seeds in the soil or potting the seedlings in the garden.

The highest rate of germination is when the soil is between the temperatures of 70 and 80°F (21–25°C), so starting them indoors is the best idea.
Sow your seeds in small seedling trays or containers such as the bottom of egg containers or milk cartons. Whatever you use, make sure there are holes in the bottom for drainage. Fill with a clean fine potting soil, peat, or compost. Do not use ordinary garden soil because it tends to get hard, and make sure your soil is light and airy enough for the little seedlings to sprout through.

After your seeds have sprouted, thin them down to two seedlings per container and let the plants spend their lives together as one plant. The leaves of two plants help protect the peppers against sunburn, and two plants together yield a much higher rate of peppers than plants on their own.

Water the seeds lightly, and keep them warm (70°F (21°C) minimum); some peppers require a heat of up to 80 to 85°F (25 to 30°C). A lower temperature means that the seedlings will take longer to germinate. At 80°F (25°C) most peppers will germinate in 10 to 15 days. At 70°F (21°C) the process will take at least 3 weeks.

Keep your planted seeds in a warm place such as above the stove or in a cupboard. They do not need light until they have already sprouted.

After they sprout, however, light is very important. A window with good lighting and lots of sun is best; if you do not have this then use artificial lighting. Regular fluorescent lights provide a cool or blue light which is fine for sprouting and growing leaves, but not for flowers or fruit. Warm or red (incandescent) light stimulates flower and fruit production but is not good for leaves, so you need a combination of the two types of light. You want to mimic sunlight, which has the full spectrum of colors. Special full-spectrum lights are available which, although expensive, last a long time (15,000 hours, or longer).

Set the lights within an inch or two of the tops of the plants, then raise them as the plants grow. Most capsicum plants need 14 to 16 hours of light a day. Pale, weak,

If you are transferring your plants outdoors, gradually allow them to get used to the outside environment to ease the process of adjustment. Start by placing them in a shaded environment and slowly expose them to more sunshine. Do not allow them to dry out or burn. After about a week they should be ready to set out in the garden; transplant them 10 to 15 in (25 to 40 cm) apart.

If you are buying established pepper plants from a garden store, choose ones with strong, green, and healthy-looking leaves. If the leaves appear pale and limp, the plants are unlikely to thrive.

If you are planting your seeds directly into the ground without starting them indoors plant them in rows after the last frost date and thin them out to 10 to 15 in (25 to 40 cm) apart once they have sprouted.

Seeds should be grown in small seedling containers, filled with potting soil.

When the seeds have sprouted, they should be thinned out into small plant containers.

Two plants together yield a higher rate of peppers than a plant on its own.

limp leaves with long delicate stems are a symptom of insufficient light.

Once your seeds have sprouted they should be fertilized. Use a half-strength solution and feed twice a week, but take care: too much nitrogen will result in large, leafy plants with no fruit.

Capsicums can be grown as houseplants, in pots in a sunny window if you do not wish to transplant them outdoors. Watch out for mites, aphids, and other pests if you grow them indoors; check the leaves and their undersides frequently, then use a damp cloth or one moistened with a small amount of soapy water, to wipe any infestation off the leaves. Use insecticides only as a last resort.

Outside, capsicums are seldom infested with pests, and indeed are often planted in a garden to keep pests away from the other plants.

Try planting the plants around cone-shaped wire cages of the type used for tomato plants — the plants grow around the cages and the peppers hang free, easy to pick and away from troubling pests or moist soil.

Peppers prefer a regular supply of water and good drainage. Too much water can make them wilt; too little water can give them blossom-end rot. It's a good idea to wait until the soil on top is dry to avoid risking fungus.

A curious fact about growing peppers: studies have shown that Epsom salts (about 1 tablespoon (15 ml) mixed in half a pint (1 L) of water) sprayed onto leaves of peppers as soon as the plants bloomed and about 10 days later, helped contribute to larger plants and fruit, due to the magnesium and salts in the Epsom salts.

Another trick: put two or three matches in the hole with each plant when you set them out. The plants like sulfur and will thrive.

about the pepper

Growing your own Chiles

Growing chiles is fun, for the sheer variety of it. Each time you see an unusual chile, pick one up, dry the seeds, and when the time comes, plant them. It's a treat to see the variety of colors, textures, heat, and flavors you will find blooming in your garden.

Chile plants start producing flowers when they are 5 to 6 in (12 to 15 cm) tall. If growing them indoors, help them to pollinate either by giving the plants a gentle shake every so often or by using a cotton swab or light brush. If you are trying to keep the varieties pure to save seeds, don't use the same brush or cotton swab on different plants.

The peppers' fire and pungency depend on the weather and sun: the hotter and brighter the sun, the spicier the pepper. A little stress on the plant, such as letting it dry just a little too far once or twice, can also increase its heat.

During the season, which will depend on the region where you live, you can pick your peppers and chiles as you like, before they grow too large, and eat them fresh. When the first frosts strike, pick the peppers that remain on the plants and dry them out for use through the winter.

A type of Thai chile, the Rooster Spur, flourishing outdoors.

A Festival

In the village of Esplette, the pepper-growing center in the Basque region of France, pepper-planting begins in mid March, traditionally on March 19, St. Joseph's Day. Within about a month the seeds have grown into tiny plants, ready to make the transition to the sunny fields. In September the ripe red peppers are harvested daily until the first frost. The peppers are strung and dried in either the warmth of the kitchen or the front of the house in the sun.

By the end of October the fête du piment, *the festival of the peppers, is celebrated with the ritual harvesting, roasting in the communal village bread ovens, and the grinding of peppers into powder. There is a ritual mass and a procession through the town, traditional Basque dancing, and a special* chanson des piments, *song of the peppers, is sung.*

Picturesque Basque country.

choosing, preparing, *and storing*

Like all fresh fruit and vegetables, freshest is best. Look for peppers that are firm, shiny, and smooth, not wrinkled, with a thick flesh and bright color. If slightly wrinkled or flabby, avoid them as they will be older and not so fresh.

All peppers start out green, unripe, then ripen on to yellow or red. A green pepper should not be too dark in color for its particular variety or it may indicate a slight immaturity without full-flavor benefits. Green peppers of all types should be picked when they reach their full size, but before they start to turn color. All peppers, sweet or hot, regardless of their color, should be free of blemishes; darkened areas on red peppers can be an indication of interior mold. Although available in stores year-round, peppers are at their best when picked at the height of their season (summer and fall).

All peppers, even fiery hot ones, are delicious eaten raw. Cut off the stems and remove the inside seeds and membranes. Some complain that raw peppers are difficult to digest; it is the skins that are hard to digest for most — peel the skin from the pepper and the problem is usually resolved.

Enjoy chopped, diced, or sliced raw peppers as a snack, as crudités, in salads or sandwiches. Raw chiles, sliced thin, are marvelous in salads, or chopped into salsas or other spicy dishes.

Choose firm fresh peppers for maximum flavor.

How to Roast and Peel Peppers and Chiles

Peeling the tough skins from peppers makes them easier to eat, and also slightly cooks the flesh, making it silky in texture. It concentrates the flavor of the pepper, giving it a more mature taste.

Heating peppers then allowing them to steam lightly loosens their skin and lets you peel it off easily, leaving a soft flesh for stuffing, puréeing in sauces and soups, slicing into pasta dishes, salads, or sandwiches. You can also blanch peppers briefly before peeling them. This results in a different, juicy texture that works well if the peppers are to be marinated or pickled. Score the skin in several places and blanch the peppers for about 2 minutes in boiling water then rinse in cold water. Peel what skin will come off easily; what remains can be peeled off with a sharp vegetable peeler.

Roasting peppers over an open flame gives the additional bonus of a smoky scent. Peppers can be roasted in a hot oven, under the broiler, or on the barbecue.

To roast peppers over an open flame on the stove, skewer them with a two-tined fork and hold them over a medium flame, turning them occasionally, until evenly charred. The skin should be blistered and blackened, but not blackened so darkly that the flesh is burnt away. Place each charred pepper in a plastic bag or wrap, a bowl, or a pan with a tight-fitting cover. Seal or cover and allow to cool for at least 10 minutes, preferably longer. They will deflate, shrivel, and look rather sad, but their skin will easily lift off, revealing a supple, silky flesh underneath.

To char peppers or chiles under the broiler, arrange them in a single layer in a baking pan or sheet. Place them under the hot broiler and allow them to char evenly, turning occasionally. Place them in a bowl or plastic bag and proceed as above.

Peppers can be successfully roasted on the dying embers of a barbecue, then placed in a covered bowl overnight. The following day they are ready to be slipped from their skins.

Main: Blanching peppers before peeling them gives them a deliciously juicy texture.
Top right: Place the roasted or charbroiled peppers in a plastic bag or covered tightly
in plastic wrap and allow them to cool.
Bottom right: Once the peppers have cooled, peel the skin from the flesh.

Storing Peppers and Chiles

Raw, unblanched peppers can be kept for about 6 months, without olive oil, between sheets of waxed paper then wrapped in plastic, in the freezer.

Roasted, peeled chiles can be frozen and kept in the freezer for up to 6 months. Their heat will fade. This is useful for whole chiles, such as poblanos or Anaheims, that may be too hot to eat. Put them in a bag and freeze for a few days to tame the fire. Defrosted peppers which have lost their flavor, on the other hand, can be boosted by sprinkling them with cayenne pepper and allowing them to marinate for a few hours.

Drying Chiles

Thread the chiles onto a length of strong white string using a large needle and a thimble to protect your thumb. Push the needle through the stem, not the flesh, of the chiles. Although it is more difficult to push through the stem, if you insert the string through the chile itself it will tend to mold and ruin the drying process.

Hang the string of large chiles in a dry hot room or on the side of a building in the sun. Tiny chiles make a charming necklace or crownlike head ornament. When I lived in Crete a neighbor's child made one for me one sunny afternoon, and it was as lovely as it was delicious when, later that winter, we plucked the dried peppers and used them to flavor our food.

How to Use Dried Chiles and Peppers

Dried chiles can be ground to a powder, soaked and the flesh scraped off, or soaked then puréed.

To serve sun-dried peppers, often from Italy or California, soak in very hot but not boiling water for 30 minutes, covered, then drain. Cut into small pieces and dress in extra-virgin olive oil with salt, minced garlic, a selection of Mediterranean herbs such as thyme, oregano, and basil, and a dash of either white wine vinegar or balsamic vinegar, or a combination of the two.

Top right: Put the fire back into defrosted chiles by sprinkling them with cayenne pepper.
Bottom right: Dried chiles on sale on a Mexican market stall.

Preserving Practicalities

You can make wonderful salsas, sauces, jellies, spreads, and pickles using peppers. However, if you want to preserve what you have made rather than eating it fresh there are strict guidelines that have to be followed.

Sterilizing

Whether bottling to keep your pickle, jelly etc. to eat as fresh or to preserve, hygiene and sanitation is essential. Make sure you use proper preserving jars. Look carefully at them and discard any that are cracked or chipped. Do not use lids that are warped or rusty, or seals that are loose and do not close properly. All of the equipment that you are going to use must be sterilized. To sterilize your jars, lids, etc. place them in a large pot and bring the water to a boil. Boil for at least 10 minutes and leave them in the water until they are needed. Dip the other utensils you will be using—tongs, knives, spoons, etc. into the boiling water for at least 30 seconds. Use the tongs to take out the jars, lids, etc. when you are ready to use them.

Fill the hot sterilized jars to within ¹/₂ inch (1 cm) of the top and using a sterilized table knife poke into the jar to release any air bubbles. Wipe the edges of the jars with a hot, damp towel, and screw the lid on tightly.

Processing

Processing pickles or preserves destroys any microorganisms and prevents spoilage. Place the filled jars in a large pot fitted with a rack for canning. Fill the pot with hot water to cover the jars by about 2 inches (5 cm) and place the lid on the pot. Bring the water to a boil and boil according to the recipe directions, adding 5 minutes for every 1,000–3,000 feet (3,000–10,000 meters) distance above sea level, up to 8,000 feet (22,000 meters).

Carefully remove the jars from the water and check to see if the jar is sealed correctly. Allow the pickles to cool completely then press the center of the lid. If the lid pops the jar did not seal and the contents should be refrigerated and eaten within 2 weeks.

Storage

Homemade preserves should always be stored in a cool dark place and let stand some weeks to allow the flavors to mature. If stored correctly most vegetable pickles maintain their crispness for up to four months and relishes keep for up to six months. Any preserve or pickle should be refrigerated after opening.

How to Pickle Peppers

Wash the peppers well, leaving the stalks and seeds intact. Arrange them in sterilized jars. Fill the jars with water, then pour off the water into a jug. Pour off half the water and replace it with vinegar. If using whole mild chiles add 4 tablespoons (60 mL) of salt. If using small hot chiles do the same. If using sweet red peppers add 3 tablespoons (45 mL) sugar and reduce the quantity of salt to 3 tablespoons (45 mL). You can either use small red peppers keeping them whole or cut large red peppers in quarters, stems and seeds removed.

Put the mixture of vinegar, water, salt, and sugar (if pickling sweet red peppers) into a nonreactive saucepan and bring to a boil. Reduce the heat, let simmer for 10 minutes, then let cool slightly for 20–30 minutes or until the liquid is warm but not hot.

Pour the warm liquid into the jars of peppers, making sure that the peppers are completely covered, then seal. After a few days check that the peppers are still completely covered, as they absorb liquid into their hollow middles. Add more vinegar if needed. They should be ready to eat in two weeks. Keep refrigerated once opened.

Pickled peppers will enhance or complement
the dish with which they are served.

a guide to sweet peppers

Mild, sweet peppers can be round, bell-shaped, heart-shaped, or long and pointed. They can be huge, as long as from your elbow to your wrist (sweet pointed peppers), or medium-sized peppers (bells), or tiny diminutive specimens such as baby peppers which can easily be mistaken for hot peppers such as habaneros, Hungarian, jalapeños, or other chiles, but are sweet and mild.

Like chiles, sweet peppers come in a riot of color: from light to dark green, bright scarlet and neon yellow, through orange, purple, lilac, white, yellow-green, brown, and black. Peppers in new colors are being grown all the time. Generally, brightly colored peppers are sweet while the dark ones are more akin to green peppers in flavor.

Green Bell Pepper

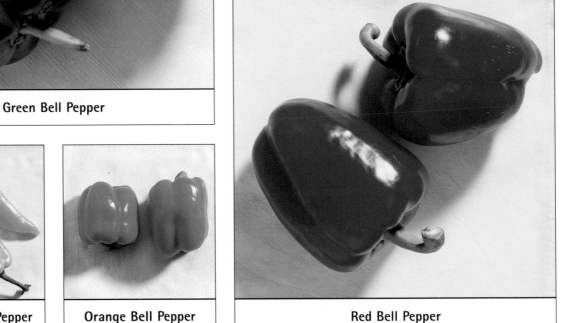

Red Bell Pepper

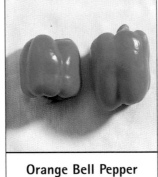

Pointed Sweet Pepper

Orange Bell Pepper

Yellow Bell Pepper

Pointed Sweet Pepper

Black Bell Pepper

Green bell peppers are mature but not quite ripe. They can have a slightly bitter, but not unpleasant flavor.

Black and purple peppers are a startling color when raw but turn dark green, like ordinary green peppers, when cooked.

Red, orange, and yellow bell peppers are very ripe, with a very sweet flavor.

Carliston biber is a pale green, fragrant mild pepper eaten in Turkey chopped in salads, barbecued whole, or pickled.

Cubanelle, Dutch long red peppers, corno di toro and Hungarian wax peppers are long, narrow peppers that are sweet and mild, though they have the appearance of a chile (see pointed sweet peppers).

Baby peppers are tiny red (and occasionally yellow and green) peppers grown for their diminutive size. These peppers can look like large jalapeños but are sweet and juicy, with a full pepper flavor. Perfect for stuffing as a garnish or appetizer, and visually very appealing.

Baby Tinkerbells are yellow mini bell peppers, similar to the baby red peppers, but these are bright yellow in color and fleshier.

Tomato peppers are similar to both tinkerbells and baby peppers but are fleshier still. They have a good strong red pepper flavor and are excellent for pickling.

Pimientos are sweet, red-fleshed peppers, usually smaller and flatter than bell peppers with a shape that is pointed at the end rather than round.

Pimiento Morron is a fleshy, bell-shaped sweet pepper eaten in Spain.

Pimiento Piquilla is the long and pointed, thin-skinned sweet red pepper of the Rioja region in Spain. Roasted over a slow wooden fire, these are traditionally bottled in jars, and eaten stuffed, in stews, warmed in olive oil, or shredded and wrapped around almost anything as a tapas.

Pointed sweet peppers are large, long, pointed sweet peppers similar in appearance to Anaheims or Hungarian mild chiles. They are green, yellow, and red, and are sweet and quite flavorful, rather like a Spanish pimiento.

About the Recipes

Notes on ingredients use and preparation:
• Medium-size vegetables and fruit should be used unless otherwise stated.
• Dried herbs should be used unless otherwise stated.
• Bell peppers should be stemmed, cored, and seeded unless other specific instructions are given in the recipe.
• Some recipes give specific instructions as to how chile peppers should be prepared, others state "1 chile pepper, chopped." In this instance the chile should, of course, be stemmed, but it is a matter of choice as to whether it is seeded and cored. Remember it is the seeds and the inner membranes that contain much of the heat.

Few flavors go as well together as peppers and garlic, therefore the recipes in this book are lavish in the amount of garlic added. Admittedly I love, adore garlic! My table reeks deliciously of the stuff. If however, you do not share my passion, or if your constitution is more delicate, or your tummy more fragile, by all means reduce the amount of garlic you add, the recipe will still be wonderful. Start with half the amount the recipe calls for and work your way up from there.

Chiles are, by and large, hot! Some are hotter than others, as noted in the introduction. You may wish to begin with a much smaller amount of chile than a recipe calls for, either to suit your milder taste or to accommodate a particularly fiery chile (this can occur unexpectedly, even in a batch of the mildest peppers).

I have given a heat rating of 1 to 5 for each recipe containing chiles or hot pepper sauces and powders. You should use this as a guideline only, to help you navigate your way through this spicy hot world. Remember however, that no one can predict the heat of any pepper; only by tasting carefully can you know for sure.

Heat rating

♠	mild, with a spicy edge
♠♠	getting spicy
♠♠♠	warm
♠♠♠♠	definitely hot
♠♠♠♠♠	very hot

how to handle the heat:
a guide to hot peppers

The Red Savina™ truly is a scorching hot pepper, measuring 350,000- 500,000 units on the Scoville heat scale.

Why Peppers are Hot

The heat of the hot pepper, or chile, comes from capsaicin, the heat-producing component of the chile. Capsaicin is measured by Scoville units, which grade heat on a scale of 0 to 500,000. To simplify things, a scale of 0-10 is usually used, with sweet peppers scoring 0 and habaneros a fiery 10. Capsaicin is said to release endorphins in the brain, which help to block pain and induce a sense of well-being, even euphoria. Many say that the experience of eating capsaicin is akin to riding a roller coaster, for the thrill of danger as you bite in and the relief when you have safely recovered. Capsaicin is also believed to enhance the libido and is regarded as an aphrodisiac.

Many recipes recommend that chile seeds be removed, to reduce the heat. While it is true that some chile seeds can be powerfully hot, I find that removing them, which is fiddly, takes some of the flavor and freshness out of the chile. The seeds have a nutty flavor and are sometimes added separately to recipes in Mexico. It is the inner membranes of the chiles which hold the seeds and stretch through the flesh of the pepper that can be intolerably hot. Scraping the seeds and membranes out of a chile can at times help to tame the heat.

Chiles can burn you, quite badly. The only guide I have to judge the heat of the pepper is to barely place the tip of my tongue – very gingerly and delicately – on the cut edge of the pepper to ascertain its fire. Since you are the one putting your tongue on the line, it is sensible to have an idea as to exactly how hot your chile might be: whether it is a jalapeño or habanero, a serrano, or a cayenne. Remember also that different parts of the chile have different levels of heat: the part closest to the stem is the hottest.

Not all chiles of the same variety that you may taste in one batch are necessarily the same: nine out of ten may be very mild but the tenth one can be so hot as to produce a blister on your lip.

Is it possible to get used to the fire of chiles? Yes. The more you eat the more you will be able to tolerate the heat, and you will be able to handle more heat the next time around. If you miss a few spicy meals, however, you are back to square one, and have to start with the milder chiles, to retrain your palate.

Warning

Never touch your face, eyes, or other sensitive areas of your body after handling chiles. Always wash your hands immediately after handling chiles, or, better still, wear rubber gloves as a protection against the burning sensation that even washing does not always remove.

What to do if your Mouth is on Fire

Whatever you do, don't reach for the water: it only spreads the capsaicin throughout your mouth. Here are a few suggested remedies: milk or dairy products are cooling. Think of yogurt or a raita with a hot curry, or sour cream on a spicy taco. Beer is cooling, rinses the volatile oils away, and also includes alcohol, which helps to dissolve the irritating oils as well as deaden the pain. Vodka, tequila, and other neutral spirits are equally effective. Sugar added to a dish that is a touch too spicy will help to reduce the heat somewhat, and a squeeze of lemon or lime juice will help to balance the palate and distract it from the heat.

Cooking with Chiles

In terms of heat, it is not only which variety of chile you choose, and the quantity you use, but also how you use it that is important. Dried chiles can be added whole to a dish such as a curry, stir-fry, or a spicy stew during cooking, then removed before serving at the end. The result will be mild, even if you use whole handfuls of chiles.

A range of ingredients that any serious chile cook should keep.

If you break the chile up, the flavor of the dish will be hotter. If you crush it the dish will be hotter still. If you grind it to a powder, this will produce the most heat. Fresh chiles are similar but slightly different in terms of the heat they produce. Their heat is more transferable because they are juicier, and their juices readily meld with whatever they are added to.

A whole chile added to a stir-fry might be fine, but add it to a stew and it will break apart, adding more fire than you might want. When you cut a fresh chile, you are breaking the cell walls that seal in the hot capsaicin juices. Slice a chile thin or chop it and whatever you add it to will be a "hot pot" indeed.

Fresh Chile Types

Very mild: Greek (green), Hungarian wax (yellow), Japanese green, Hungarian sweet cherry peppers, Dutch red or green chiles and pale green to yellow-orange banana chiles which are so mild the inside is often rubbed with a hot chile to impart more heat.

Mild to medium-hot: poblanos, Anaheims, Korean green (much like a large and milder cayenne or a spicy, thin Turkish pepper), Esplette (red), Turkish, crimson hot (smaller and more piquant than an Anaheim, larger and milder than a jalapeño), Chimayo, Hungarian hot cherry peppers: round and brownish red in color with a spicy flavor, often sold in strands to be picked off as required. Yellow-heart chiles are much like Hungarian wax peppers, and can be very bland but are attractive to look at.

Medium-hot: jalapeños, Kenya, Fresno, aji, Turkish chiles (twisted bright green, red, pale green); de agua chiles are long and either green or red.

Hot: Congo chile, also grown in Mombasa and Zanzibar: small, green turning red, very hot. Fresh aji (yellow in color, eaten throughout South America, especially in Peru), hot peppers eaten in Cuba and throughout South America; Malagueta, the fiery cousin of tabasco; serranos, the most easily found fresh hot chile in America and Mexico: smallish, long, and round-nosed, either green or red; cayenne peppers are probably the most widespread chile in the world, not too fleshy or juicy, but hot and hearty. Cayenne peppers can range from tiny miniature ones to large, long ones. "Rat's turds" or "mouse droppings" are tiny, round berrylike chiles, with a distinctive, almost habanero-scent to match their heat. Lilac bird's eyes are beautiful: lilac and pale purple when unripe, a striking lilac-orange-red hue when they ripen. Diavoletti, Calabrian for "little devils," these small round chiles, about $3/4$ inch (2 cm) in length, are sold in olive oil, on their own, or stuffed with anchovies and capers. They are pleasingly hot.

Very hot: habanero, Scotch bonnets, bird's eye, Chinese lantern, Thai, the round apple-shaped Rocoto and the longer oblong-shaped Rocatillo (also known as aji cachucha), as well as the incendiary tiny, little round berrylike chiles.

Hungarian Wax

Sweet Cherry

Anaheim

Yellow Heart

Jalapeño

Serrano

Habanero

Thai

Chiles drying outside a store in Scottsdale, Arizona.

Dried Chiles

These can be seen hanging whole outside adobe huts throughout New Mexico and Arizona: Chimayo chiles are the most prized, vibrantly colored and fiery in the desert landscape. In Esplette, France, peppers are also dried on the walls of the Mediterranean stone houses. Esplette is famous for its annual chile festival (p.14).

Mild: dark and wrinkled large chiles, such as ancho, mulatto, negro; These are thick-skinned, some with an almost flexible leathery texture, and prunelike, chocolate flavors. They are generally, but not always, quite mild. Their distinctive earthy flavor is the main ingredient that sets mild chili powder apart from other hot pepper mixtures. Sometimes a wrinkled mild dark-hued chile might be called pasilla. Smooth, large red chiles such as New Mexico, California, pasilla, Chimayo, guajillo, and pulla; Nura or Nora (known as romesco in Catalonia) is a European Spanish/southern French chile that has a mild ancholike flavor but is slightly smaller, and Esplette is a bright red, mild chile with a distinctive flavor, from the Basque region. Guindilla is a small hot chile from northwestern Spain, much like cayenne. Choricero is a Rioja chile, much like the Nura, and the Turkish Kirmizi biber is a similar pepper.

Round, moderately mild chiles: cascabel, also known as the rattlesnake chile because of the rattling sound the seeds make inside the peppers. Hungarian hot cherry peppers are similar, with a nice heat and a rich roasted flavor, with almost chocolatelike overtones.

Small medium to hot chiles: these can be added whole to a sauce, or crumbled into flakes; Kashmir, also known as Sracha, is related to the jalapeño and serrano; available green or red, they are made into a sauce in Thailand. Prik chee fa are also Thai chiles, red and fat in shape and not as hot as other Thai chiles. Kalyanpur, Kesankurru, and kovilpatt are all Indian chiles of varying heat levels eaten throughout the country.

Hot chiles: hontaka or Honka: Japanese red or orange chiles, dried and wrinkled. Santaka chiles are a red Japanese pepper. Dried cayenne, tabasco, and bird's eye are a few of the best-known of these hot chiles, though pequin, tepin, dried aji, are all found in markets depending on where you find yourself. Arbol or de Arbol are fiery and delicious added to soups or pickles.

Very hot chiles: the Argentinian aji p-p, otherwise known as the "bad word chile" or putapario, a pepper so fiery that the legendary first eater felt like screaming obscenities. The Jamaican habaneros, too, are as hot as it gets; they are sold fresh or dried.

Smoked chiles: the most famous is the fragrant hot chipotles, the dried ripe jalapeño. Other types of smoked chiles include: Guatemalan cobans (a piquin), moritas (a milder type of jalapeño), as well as a wide variety of smoked chiles such as those you would find in Oaxaca, Mexico (often a mulatto or negro).

Hot Cherry

Hot Kashmir

Birds Eye

Habanero

about the pepper

How to grind chiles into powder

Lightly roast the dried chiles over an open flame, under the broiler, or in a hot oven. Turn once or twice for even roasting, taking care not to burn the chiles, or they will acquire an acrid, unpleasant flavor. Allow the chiles to cool slightly, remove their skins and stems, and break up the chiles into smallish pieces. Place these in a cleaned coffee grinder and process to a fine powder. Store in tightly sealed jars. (To clean the coffee grinder, wipe clean with a damp cloth, then whirl several tablespoons of raw rice through the grinder until it is pulverized. Pour it out, wipe the inside of the grinder clean again, then use.)

How to rehydrate chiles

Lightly roast the chiles over an open flame or in an ungreased hot skillet until just fragrant, only a few moments, then place them in a saucepan or deep bowl. Pour boiling water over them, cover, and allow to soak for at least 1 hour, turning them once or twice so they are evenly submerged in the water. Remove the peppers from the water, remove their seeds and stems, then, using a paring knife, lightly scrape the flesh from the skin. Discard the skin and use the flesh as desired. This makes a very fine, flavorful mild chile purée.

Powdered Peppers

Aleppo pepper: Syrian hot pepper with a fine strong flavor. As a substitute, use a combination of about two-thirds paprika and one-third cayenne pepper.

Ancho: deliciously rich, mild, and flavorful, the basis for Mexican moles and mild chili powder.

Berebere: Ethiopian hot pepper: a mixture of chile and spices such as ginger, cardamom, paprika, and others.

Caribe: not too hot, but full of flavor, this bright red chili powder is from New Mexico.

Cayenne pepper: Also known as hot pepper. Crushed small hot peppers are usually of the cayenne type.

Hot pepper flakes: cayenne pepper crushed into small pieces rather than a fine powder. Hot pepper flakes are good in pizza, sandwiches, or whenever you want a hot pepper flavor.

Hot paprika: powdered spicy peppers, not as hot as cayenne or other chiles. Hot paprika can be adjusted to your own taste by mixing a combination of paprika and cayenne.

Kirmizi Biber: Turkish red pepper powder, it can be sweet and mild, or hot and spicy, and is sold in a variety of these pungencies. They can be sold in flakes or ground to a powder (*pul biber*) and vary in color from bright scarlet to deep purplish-brownish red. Kirmizi biber is usually oiled; this oiling not only seals in the flavor and heat but also helps to impart the flavor when it is added to food. Sometimes it is roasted after oiling, until it has an almost smoky flavor, and a dark color. This oiling, and roasting after oiling, is unusual and differs from the treatment of chiles and peppers in the cuisines of other cultures.

Mulatto: darker than ancho with an even deeper flavor. Use as you would ancho.

Pasilla powder: dark, fruity, a great all-round mild chili powder.

Pimenton de la Vera: Spanish sweet paprika/chili powder with a smoky flavor.

Pimenton fuerte: hot, Spanish pepper. Cayenne is a good substitute, or a mixture of cayenne and paprika.

Pimenton dulce (in the north of Spain) or **Colorado** (south of Spain): paprika.

Paprika: The ground dried red mild pepper. Hungarian paprika, especially rose paprika, has a strong sweet pepper flavor.

Piri-piri: hot peppery condiment from Portugal and Africa. Classic with chicken.

Bottled and Pickled Peppers

Wherever you go in the world there is a pickle, chutney, or relish to complement your meal. Many of these contain peppers and chiles – hot vegetable pickles from the Middle East, spicy relishes of south-east Asia, chile paste from China, and flavorful preserves made from the sun-kissed ingredients of the Mediterranean. They can be used to add flavor to sauces and marinades, smeared onto meats and fish, and added to soups and stir-fries. Most of these products are available to buy in specialty food stores or large supermarkets.

Caribbean hot sauces: based on the habanero, these sauces are extremely hot with the distinctive perfume of the habanero or Scotch bonnet.

Chili paste (or garlic-chili paste, either Chinese or Vietnamese): this fiery, flavorful paste is an essential addition to the spice rack. Smear it onto meats, dab it into noodle soups, add it to stir-fries. It is marvelous and well worth seeking out.

Fire-roasted red (and red/yellow) peppers: easily available, from the Mediterranean and California.

Harissa: North African hot pepper paste made from puréed peppers and spices. Use fresh or dried, simmered and puréed chiles, or buy the paste in a jar. Most harissa is flavored with caraway seeds; I find the addition of chopped garlic, cumin, lemon juice, and a little olive oil or chopped cilantro at the last minute refreshes the sauce delightfully.

Jalapeños en escabeche: pickled jalapeños (or serranos), Mexican-style, are sold in nearly any supermarket in Mexico, most of North America, and increasingly in other parts of the world too. If these are not available, make your own: see Pickled Green Chiles (p. 136).

Pickled peppers: large red sweet peppers are often available from Eastern European countries where they are bottled in lightly sweetened and salted vinegar. If you have a chance to sample Sauerkraut-stuffed spicy yellow peppers from Bulgaria, don't miss out on the opportunity, they are delicious. Turkish and Greek pickled chiles and

peppers range from mild to quite spicy, and sampling is the only way to find the difference. **Jalapeños en escabeche** or **jalapeño chiles** are often preserved in vinegar with other vegetables, and **chipotles en adobo** are smoked chiles simmered in a spicy, smoky sauce. These are good with most Mexican dishes.

Siracha: A Thai bottled all-purpose hot sauce, spicy and delicious with fish.

Bottled/canned pimientos: available either plain, in a light brine, or simmered into a preparation such as the Hungarian Lesco, or stew of peppers that is added to all manner of their dishes.

Piquillos: a descendant of the first Spanish peppers grown from the seeds that Columbus brought back from the New World, the piquillo first appeared in the early twentieth century in Navarre in Spain. Now a classic of the Spanish kitchen, they are exported throughout the world. Piquillo peppers are smallish and richly red-fleshed, with a smoky scent that comes from slow-roasting over a wood fire.

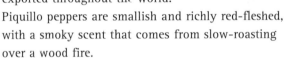

Salsas: innumerable varieties of excellent Mexican salsas and hot pepper sauces are available. Taste your way through the range.

Turkish Hot Pepper Paste: delicious and hot enough to thrill but not usually enough to maim. It is tasty rather than painful, and delicious eaten on its own, added to other dishes or marinades for meats.

World Guide to Chiles

This map, though not exhaustive, shows where chiles are grown throughout the world.

Key:

North and Central America
1. California (USA)
2. Arizona (USA)
3. Baja California (USA)
4. New Mexico (USA)
5. Texas (USA)
6. Florida (USA)
7. Mexico
8. Guatemala / El Salvador / Belize
9. Honduras
10. Panama
11. Caribbean Islands, particularly Jamaica

South America
12. Venezuela
13. Peru
14. Brazil
15. Bolivia
16. Argentina
17. Chile

Europe
18. Spain
19. France
20. Italy
21. Hungary
22. Greece
23. Turkey

Africa
24. Morocco
25. Tunisia
26. Libya
27. Eritrea
28. Ethiopia
29. Kenya
30. Tanzania
31. Congo

Asia
32. Israel
33. Yemen
34. India
35. China (Hunan and Szechwan provinces)
36. Laos
37. Vietnam
38. Cambodia
39. Indonesia
40. Thailand
41. Myanmar (Burma)
42. Japan

what to drink with peppers

The strong flavors of peppers and chiles present challenges in choosing what to drink alongside.

Dishes based on sweet peppers are not too difficult to partner. Many of the Mediterranean cuisines offer marvelous wines that set off the flavor of the pepper. Think of Provence, with its delicate rosés or intense Rhônes, or Italy with its refreshing Frascati and full-bodied Barolo or robust Valpolicella.

Hot peppers are more of a problem. Try taking a cue from the originating cuisines: Mexican food, and Indian food too, go very well with chilled beer, and both are difficult to pair with a wine that will stand up happily to the heat. If opting for wine, a hint (or more than a hint) of sweetness is appreciated, as is a chill in the temperature, for the chill is refreshing and the sugar helps to temper the heat. For this reason,

many spicy dishes are more successfully partnered by a light, vivacious refreshing white wine than a tannin-rich and robust red. Riesling, Gewürtztraminer, and Chenin Blanc stand up very well to many spicy foods, especially Hungarian pepper-rich stews and dishes flavored with paprika, but drier white wines such as Orvieto, white Rioja, and Chardonnay, are not so successful. Some Merlots, Cabernets Sauvignons, and Zinfandels can handle the heat — taste until you find a favorite.

Tequila is, of course, the drink of the day when you think of Mexican food. There is a good reason for this: its high alcohol content numbs the pain receptors and dulls the heat of the chiles.

Chilled fruit juices, diluted with lots of ice or iced water, with the addition of a few fresh herbs, make a refreshing accompaniment to most spicy foods. Apple, pineapple, cherry, and mango juice are all equally refreshing. Cider, too, is as refreshing as beer, and its slight fruitiness is welcome.

The Mexicans make a marvelous punch that consists of fresh fruit juice, sliced cucumber, and mint. Iced tea is also good if your mouth feels on fire. In Southeast Asia sweet, milky iced tea or iced coffee is often drunk; here, too, the coolness is refreshing and the sweetness soothing to the mouth, and the milk helps to reduce the irritation caused by the heat.

Left: A cool beer is a great partner with tortilla chips and fiery salsas.
Above: A dish containing sweet peppers can be complemented with a robust Valpolicella.

soups & appetizers

Peppers make up the supporting flavors for many of the world's soups but they can also be the subject of the soup itself: sweet and puréed, or chunky and coarse-textured.

louisiana mixed *pepper gumbo*

This Louisiana dish traditionally uses a variety of different peppers, but if you only have one or two types on hand, the dish will be just as successful. Smoked sausage gives the gumbo a rich flavor; for a more upmarket gumbo add seafood, as much as you like.

Serves 6

1 mild green chile, whole
1 onion, chopped
1 stalk celery, chopped
1 Tbsp (15 mL) fresh chopped
   parsley
2 Tbsp (25 mL) extra-virgin
   olive oil
1 each: red and green bell
   pepper, mild green pepper,
   long yellow pepper, wax
   pepper, sliced
5 to 8 cloves garlic, chopped
½ tsp (2 mL) each: cumin,
   paprika, thyme, onion powder
⅛ tsp (0.5 mL) fresh cilantro
1 kielbasa smoked sausage
   (approx 6 oz/175–200 g), cut
   into bite-sized pieces
2 Tbsp (25 mL) all-purpose
   flour
1 quart (1 L) hot vegetable,
   fish, beef, ham, duck,
   or chicken broth
1 lb (500 g) ripe tomatoes,
   diced, or 14-oz (398-mL) can
   tomatoes, diced, plus their
   juices
3 fresh bay leaves, whole
3 to 5 small to medium-sized
   okra, thinly sliced
Black pepper and salt
1 small bunch scallions,
   chopped (optional)

Preparation time: 20 minutes Cooking time: 30–40 minutes

Roast the mild chile over an open flame until charred and blackened; peel off the skin. Try not to rinse it – you will lose the nice smoky flavor. Discard the stems and seeds and coarsely chop the flesh.

Sauté the onion, celery, and parsley until softened, then add the reserved hot roasted chile and all of the other peppers and chiles. Cook over a moderate heat, stirring, until softened, then sprinkle in the spices. Add the sausage, then the flour, and cook for a few moments over medium-high heat.

Remove from the heat and pour in the broth, stirring as it bubbles and thickens, then return to the heat and add the tomatoes, bay leaves, and okra. Simmer for about 10 minutes or until the soup is thick and flavorful. Remove the bay leaves now or from the individual serving bowls.

Season with black pepper and salt if needed, and serve in bowls with spoonfuls of cooked rice, and a sprinkling of chopped scallions if liked. You can garnish with bay leaves, but these should be discarded before eating.

soups &
appetizers

louisiana mixed pepper gumbo

yellow pepper *soup with pistou*

This soup is stylish, and simple to prepare — after you've sautéed the peppers, reserve a small amount and pound into a paste or pistou, along with bits of tomatoes and herbs. Use whatever herb is available, keeping in mind the Mediterranean flavors of the other ingredients.

Serves 4

3 yellow bell peppers, chopped

1 onion, chopped

¼ cup (25–45 mL) olive oil

6 cloves garlic, chopped

1 large potato, diced

1 quart (1 L) chicken or
   vegetable broth (or water
   mixed with 2 bouillon cubes)

Large pinch mixed herbs or
   1 Tbsp (15 mL) fresh,
   chopped thyme

Salt and pepper to taste

1 lb (500 g) ripe tomatoes,
   diced, including the juices,
   or 14-oz (398-mL) can
   tomatoes, including the juices

2–3 Tbsp (25–45 mL) fresh,
   chopped mint or basil leaves

Preparation time: 20 minutes   Cooking time: 20 minutes

Lightly sauté the peppers with the onions in about 2 tablespoons of the olive oil until the peppers are soft. Reserve about 3 tablespoons of the peppers from the saucepan to make the pistou.

Add about half of the garlic, the potato, broth, and dried herbs or thyme, and salt and pepper to the peppers and onion in the pot. If using fresh tomatoes, add them now, reserving about 3 tablespoons for the pistou. (If using canned tomatoes, add when you purée the mixture in a few minutes.)

Bring to a boil, reduce the heat, cover, and simmer until the potato is soft. Meanwhile, make the pistou: combine the reserved pepper with the remaining 3 tablespoons finely chopped tomatoes, the reserved garlic, the reserved olive oil, and the fresh herbs. Mix well and set aside.

If using canned tomatoes, add them now. Purée the solid ingredients in the soup with just enough liquid to obtain a smooth purée then return to the saucepan with the remaining liquid and heat through. Season to taste.

Serve the soup hot, and top each portion with a spoonful of pistou mixture stirred in at the last moment.

apache *soup*

This filling soup, which can also be served as a stew, is a favorite Apache recipe.

It combines the native American traditions of hunting and gathering,

being traditionally made with venison or other game, hominy, and whatever

wild greens could be found in the fields.

Preparation time: 20–25 minutes Cooking time: 1–1½ hours

Lightly brown the lamb, onion, and half the garlic in the oil; add extra oil if needed, but avoid using too much (traditionally, Apaches did not fry, so their dishes are never greasy).

Add the peppers, chiles, carrot, cumin, and tomatoes and cook for a few minutes, then add the broth, mint, and hominy, and bring to a boil. Reduce the heat and cook at a low simmer for about 30 minutes or until the meat and vegetables are tender.

Just before serving season to taste then add the greens at the last moment, allowing them to wilt briefly in the heat of the pot. Serve each bowlful with lemon wedges if wished.

Serves 4

5 oz (150 g) lean lamb or beef, shredded
1 onion, chopped
5 to 8 cloves garlic, sliced thin
1 tsp (5 mL) oil
1 each: red and green bell pepper, roasted, peeled, and chopped fine
1 each: mild red and mild green chile, peeled and diced
1 large carrot, sliced thin
½ tsp (2 mL) cumin
4 ripe tomatoes, diced
6¼ cups (1.5 L) beef, lamb, or vegetable broth
½ tsp (2 mL) mint
14 oz (400 g) cooked and drained hominy (or use canned)
4–5 oz (100–150 g) leaves or greens, torn
Salt and pepper
Lemon wedges (optional)

gulyas *soup*

This Hungarian dish can be a sauce or stew or soup depending on how

thick it is and which ingredients are included. Add a spoonful

of cooked rice or noodles to each serving, and top with a little yogurt.

Preparation time: 10–15 minutes Cooking time: 2 hours

Sauté the onion, carrot, bell pepper, and garlic in the oil until lightly softened, then sprinkle in the flour and cook for a few minutes. Stir well, then sprinkle in the paprika and allow this to cook for a few minutes as well, to eliminate its raw flavor.

Stir in the tomatoes, broth, potatoes, bay leaves, thyme, salt, and pepper, and bring to a boil over high heat. When it reaches a boil, reduce the heat, cover, and cook at a low simmer for about 2 hours or until it is richly flavored and thickened, and slightly reduced in volume. Check about halfway through the cooking time and if it seems too watery, continue cooking uncovered. Once ready you can remove the bay leaves from the pan or after you have served. Season to taste.

Serves 4 to 6

1 large onion, chopped
1 large carrot, sliced
1 green bell pepper, chopped
5 cloves garlic, chopped
3–5 Tbsp (45–65 mL) vegetable or olive oil
2 Tbsp (25 ml) all-purpose flour
5 Tbsp (65 mL) paprika
4 ripe tomatoes, coarsely chopped
4½ pt (2 L) broth of choice
3 to 4 medium-sized potatoes, peeled and diced
3 fresh bay leaves
¼–½ tsp fresh or dried thyme
Salt and pepper

red pepper soup *with Provençal flavors*

This vibrantly colored soup, from the South of France,

is scented with the Provençal flavors of garlic, tomatoes, fennel, and herbs.

If the weather is hot, serve it chilled rather than hot.

Serves 4

5 shallots, chopped

3 cloves garlic, chopped

2 Tbsp (25 mL) olive oil

2 red bell peppers, chopped

9 oz (250 g) tomatoes, chopped
(or half a 14-oz (398-mL)
can tomatoes, including
the juices)

1 Tbsp (15 mL) Pernod or Ouzo,
if preferred a pinch of anise
or fennel seeds can be added

2 tsp (10 mL) tsp paprika

$^1/_2$ tsp (2 mL) herbes de
Provence

2$^1/_4$ cups (500 mL) chicken or
vegetable broth

1 cup (250 mL) sour cream

Fresh thyme sprig to garnish

Preparation time: 15 minutes Cooking time: 30–35 minutes

Lightly sauté the shallots and garlic in the olive oil until soft, then add the peppers and cook over medium-low heat until the peppers are soft.

Add the tomatoes, Pernod, paprika, herbes de Provence, and broth and cook over medium-high heat until mixture comes to a boil.

Purée the soup, leaving a little texture of the red peppers to the mixture. Stir half the sour cream into a bowl then add several spoonfuls of the soup to it, mixing until smooth. Add this mixture to the soup, keeping it on the heat just long enough to warm it through.

Serve garnished with a spoonful of the remaining sour cream and a sprig of thyme.

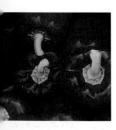

soups &
appetizers

tropical chile *coconut soup*

Guajillos are chiles with a fruity warmth rather than a fiery heat. This spicy soup is balanced by the addition of sweet tropical fruit. To counteract the heat, you can add a scoop of cooked rice to each serving.

Preparation time: 20 minutes Cooking time: 20 minutes

Place the guajillo or other dried chiles in a bowl and pour hot water over them. Allow to soak until softened, about 30 minutes. Remove the stems and seeds then cut the chiles into small pieces. Purée in a blender or food processor using just enough of the soaking liquid to make a purée.

Roast the onion and garlic cloves in a heavy ungreased skillet until lightly charred. When cool enough to handle, peel the onion and garlic and coarsely chop. Combine them with the paprika, half the tomatoes, and the chile purée. Purée until smooth.

Heat the oil in a saucepan. Add the purée and cook until it concentrates and becomes dark in color and pastelike in texture. Do not allow to burn.

Add the chicken broth, zucchini, and pepper. Bring to a boil then reduce the heat and cook until the zucchini are tender. Add the coconut milk, oregano, and cumin. Heat through, then season with salt and pepper.

Serve hot with a sprinkling of banana, lime, the remaining tomato, and cilantro.

Serves 4

1 to 2 guajillo chiles, whole
1 onion, unpeeled, cut
  crosswise into half
5 cloves garlic, unpeeled
1 tsp (5 mL) paprika
10 oz (300 g) tomatoes, diced
1 Tbsp (15 mL) vegetable oil
3 cups (750 mL) chicken broth
1 zucchini, cut into bite-sized
  pieces
1 yellow bell pepper, diced
1 cup (250 mL) coconut milk
  (or a 2–3 inch piece creamed
  coconut, shredded into 1 cup
  (250 mL) hot water)
Large pinch oregano
Large pinch cumin
Salt and pepper
½ ripe but firm banana, diced
1 lime, cut into wedges
1 Tbsp (15 mL) fresh chopped
  cilantro

moroccan pepper *and tomato soup*

Known as *Shlada* in Morocco, this chilled, spiced soup, which is similar to Gazpacho, is made of pounded roasted green bell peppers and juicy tomatoes. *Shlada* may also be prepared quite thick and eaten as a sauce or salsa to accompany meat kabobs.

Preparation time: 20–25 minutes

Purée the garlic and peppers until thick and saucelike in consistency. Add the tomatoes, broth, cumin, lemon juice, olive oil, salt, and cayenne to taste and mix gently until evenly amalgamated.

Stir in the cucumber, and float some crushed ice cubes in each serving.

Serves 4

3 garlic cloves, minced
2 green bell peppers, roasted,
  peeled, and diced
14 oz (400 g) tomatoes, diced
  (or 14-oz (398-mL) can
  tomatoes, including the juices)
3 cups (750 mL) chicken or
  vegetable broth
¼ tsp (1 mL) cumin
Juice of ½ lemon, or to taste
1 Tbsp (15 mL) extra-virgin
  olive oil
Salt and cayenne pepper
½ cucumber, peeled, seeded,
  and diced
8 ice cubes, broken or crushed

pepper *and eggplant pâté*

Serves 4

1 each: red, orange, yellow bell
   pepper, diced
3 Tbsp (45 mL) extra-virgin
   olive oil
4 to 5 cloves garlic, sliced thin
Salt to taste
1 eggplant
Black and cayenne pepper
   to taste
½ tsp (2 mL) lemon juice, or
   to taste
Few sprigs of fresh parsley
   to garnish

Known in its native Bulgaria as *Ajvar*, this reddish-colored pâté derives its creamy consistency and smoked flavor from the fire-roasted eggplant. Serve with a selection of crudités such as cucumbers, scallions, or sweet peppers.

Preparation time: 30 minutes Cooking time: 30 minutes

Sweat the peppers in the olive oil, then add the garlic and salt to taste. When the peppers are very soft remove from the heat.

Meanwhile, roast the eggplant, either in the oven (preheat oven to 400°F/200°C), or, for a richer flavor, over a gas flame or on a barbecue. Turn the eggplant occasionally to char the vegetable evenly and when it appears to have deflated from the inside transfer it to a bowl and cover it. Allow to cool, about 30 minutes.

Remove the skin from the eggplant, reserving the juices, and dice the flesh.

Return the peppers to the heat and add the eggplant flesh and the juices. Cook over medium-low heat for 5 to 8 minutes or until the mixture loses some of its moisture and thickens slightly.

Purée the vegetable mixture in a blender or food processor, then season with black and cayenne pepper, and lemon juice to taste. Season to taste and serve garnished with sprigs of parsley.

feta cheese pâté *with roasted red peppers*

Tender peppers paired with a strong-flavored mixture of feta cheese, garlic, and olive oil makes a marvelous summer appetizer, especially if the meal is barbecued. It can be made in advance and, if you prefer a more colorful dish, substitute one or two of the red peppers for green or yellow ones.

Preparation time: 20 minutes

Combine the feta cheese with the garlic, oregano, yogurt, and 2 tablespoons olive oil. Season to taste. Serve the cheese mixture surrounded by the peppers drizzled with the remaining olive oil and some balsamic vinegar.

Serves 4

5 oz (150 g) feta cheese, crumbled

3 cloves garlic, chopped

¼ tsp (1 mL) oregano

2 Tbsp (25 mL) yogurt

6 Tbsp (75 mL) extra-virgin olive oil

3 red bell peppers, roasted, peeled, and cut into large slices

Balsamic vinegar to taste

andalucian roasted peppers *with garlic*

This tapas of silky peppers is marvelous eaten with crisp toasts, drizzled with lots of garlic-flavored olive oil. Rub the toasts with raw garlic before you lay the pepper piece on top. Serve with some ham and a bowl of green olives.

Preparation time: 15 minutes Cooking time: 30 minutes

Place the peppers in a large, heavy skillet with the sliced garlic and the olive oil. Sprinkle with salt, and cover. Cook gently, covered, for about 20 minutes over very low heat, turning once or twice.

When the peppers are very tender, remove the lid, and increase the heat to medium-high. Add the balsamic vinegar, then remove from the heat and add the white wine vinegar. Pour into a bowl and allow to cool. When cold, add more salt and wine vinegar if wished.

Serves 4

3 each: red and yellow bell peppers, roasted, peeled, and cut into bite-sized pieces

15 to 20 cloves garlic, sliced thin

½ cup (100 mL) extra-virgin olive oil

Salt to taste

Balsamic vinegar to taste

White wine vinegar to taste

pepper *and tomato bruschetta*

Serves 4 to 6

4 small to medium-sized
   tomatoes
Salt to taste
Pinch sugar
2 Tbsp (25 mL) extra-virgin
   olive oil
4 red bell peppers, roasted,
   peeled, and diced
2 to 3 cloves garlic, chopped
Few drops of white wine
   vinegar or balsamic vinegar,
   to taste
Few fresh basil leaves, torn, or
   other sweet Mediterranean
   herb such as oregano or
   marjoram

Serve this bright red mixture of roasted tomatoes and peppers on crisply toasted bread that has been rubbed with a clove of garlic. This Italian hors d'oeuvre can be followed by a main course of broiled sardines, roasted chicken, or pasta.

Preparation time: 15 minutes Cooking time: 15–20 minutes

Cut the tomatoes crosswise into half and sprinkle the cut half lightly with salt and a tiny amount of sugar.

Heat a tablespoon of the olive oil in a heavy skillet just large enough to take all the tomato halves. When the skillet is hot, place the tomatoes skin-side down and cook for a few minutes over high heat until the tomatoes are charred underneath, then turn them carefully, reduce the heat to about medium-high, and cook, covered, until done. Do not overcook. Remove from the heat and leave, covered, until cool.

Dice the roasted tomatoes and combine them, with their juices, with the diced peppers and garlic. Season with salt, and add the vinegar and remaining olive oil. Serve at room temperature, sprinkled with the herbs.

moroccan-style *broiled peppers and tomatoes*

Serves 4

4 green bell peppers, halved
2 Tbsp (25 mL) extra-virgin
   olive oil
2 onions, sliced thin
Salt to taste
2 lb (1 kg) tomatoes, diced
Pinch sugar

Broiled peppers have a deliciously smoky, slightly bitter flavor — which blends very well with the sweet freshness of tomatoes in this saladlike appetizer.

Preparation time: 15–20 minutes Cooking time: 20–30 minutes

Place the peppers skin-side down in hot olive oil and cook over medium-high heat until they char slightly, then turn them over and add the onions and salt. Continue to cook and when the onions are lightly browned add the tomatoes and sugar. Cook over medium high heat, turning occasionally, until the tomatoes are reduced and thickened to a rich saucelike consistency.

Serve at room temperature.

pepper and tomato bruschetta

pepper *and olive salad*

Serves 6

2 small to medium-sized onions,
 chopped
2 each: red, green, yellow bell
 peppers, cut into bite-sized
 pieces
1 to 2 mild green chiles,
 sliced (optional)
5 to 7 cloves garlic, chopped
6 Tbsp (75 mL) extra-virgin
 olive oil
¼ tsp (1 mL) each: curry
 powder, turmeric, dried ginger
Seeds from 2 to 3 cardamom
 pods or a pinch ground
 cardamom
½ tsp (2 mL) cumin
1–1¼ lb (500–600 g) tomatoes,
 diced or (14-oz (398-mL) can
 tomatoes, chopped)
Pinch sugar
Salt and pepper
1 medium bottle green pimiento-
 stuffed olives, drained
6 Tbsp (75 mL) fresh chopped
 cilantro
Juice of ½ lemon

This can be served as a salad, a sauce, even a spread. It is delicious as part of a selection of salad appetizers, or as an accompaniment to boiled potatoes, tuna fish, and ripe tomato wedges. Interestingly, this salad is a favorite in Israel, but it actually originates in Turkey.

Preparation time: 20–25 minutes Cooking time: 20–30 minutes

Lightly sauté the onions, peppers, chiles (if using) and garlic in the olive oil until they are softened and lightly browned, about 15 minutes, stirring occasionally.

Sprinkle in the curry powder and other spices, stir and cook for a few minutes to draw out the flavors, then add the tomatoes and continue to cook until thickened.

Season to taste with sugar, salt, and pepper, and stir in the olives and cilantro. Pour over the lemon juice and stir gently. Chill until ready to serve.

roasted peppers *with yogurt and mint*

Serves 4

1½ each: red and green bell
 peppers, roasted, peeled,
 and diced
2 Tbsp (25 mL) extra-virgin
 olive oil
Salt and cayenne pepper
 to taste
4 cloves garlic, chopped fine
12 oz (350 g) Balkan yogurt
2 Tbsp (25 mL) fresh chopped
 mint leaves

Serve this Turkish appetizer, *Salata Filfil be Laban*, with bread for dipping and a bowl of olives. It also makes a good accompaniment to broiled lamb kabobs.

Preparation time: 15 minutes Cooking time: 15 minutes

Lightly sauté the roasted diced peppers in the olive oil until they soften; do not allow to brown. Sprinkle with salt and pepper and half the garlic as the peppers cook.

Remove from the heat and mix in the yogurt, remaining garlic, and mint. Chill until ready to serve.

turkish roasted red peppers *and eggplant*
in cumin-scented yogurt

Serves 4

1 small to medium-sized
  eggplant, sliced thick
Salt
5 Tbsp (65 mL) extra-virgin
  olive oil, or to taste
2 to 3 red bell peppers, roasted,
  peeled, and diced
Cayenne pepper to taste
4 cloves garlic, chopped fine
1½ cups (350 mL) yogurt
Pinch cumin
Juice of ½ lemon
Fresh flat leaf parsley
  to garnish

Another refreshing appetizer of roasted peppers and yogurt, this one is rich with roasted eggplant and lightly spiced with cumin.

It can also be served as an accompaniment to barbecued lamb.

Preparation time: 15–20 minutes Cooking time: 15–20 minutes

Generously sprinkle the eggplant with salt and leave for at least 30 minutes. Rinse well and pat dry, then brown in about 2 tablespoons of the olive oil, adding more if needed. Remove from the heat when the eggplant is tender and lightly browned, cut into small pieces.

Meanwhile, dice the roasted red peppers and toss them with the remaining olive oil, and salt and cayenne pepper to taste. Mix the peppers with the garlic and yogurt, then stir in the eggplant, cumin, and lemon juice. Taste for seasoning and chill until ready to serve. Garnish with flat leaf parsley.

spiced green pepper salad *with tomatoes, cumin, and garlic*

Another North African salad combining peppers and tomatoes.

Here the peppers are sautéed with mild chiles and tomatoes.

Serve as an appetizer or accompaniment to couscous.

Preparation time: 15 minutes Cooking time: 20–30 minutes ♀♀♀

Place the peppers and chiles skin-side down in hot olive oil and cook over medium-high heat until they char slightly, then turn them over and add the onions and salt.

Continue to cook and when the onions are lightly browned add the tomatoes, sugar, and cumin. Cook over medium high heat, turning occasionally, until the tomatoes are thickened and saucelike, having reduced to a rich intense flavor, then stir in the garlic.

Serve at room temperature as a saladlike appetizer.

Serves 4

4 green bell peppers, cut into quarters or thick slices

2 large mild chiles such as poblano or Anaheim, cut into strips

2 Tbsp (25 mL) extra-virgin olive oil

2 onions, sliced thin

Salt to taste

2 lb (1 kg) tomatoes, diced (or 2 x 14-oz (398-mL) cans tomatoes)

Pinch sugar

1/2–1 tsp (2–5 mL) cumin

2 to 3 cloves garlic, chopped

peruvian-style *red snapper seviche*

Seviche is a dish of marinated fish, popular throughout Latin America.

Seviche always includes chiles, and usually sweet peppers too.

Serve spooned onto lettuce leaves, or, as they do in Peru, accompany each

portion with a chunk of cold cooked corn on the cob or sweet potato.

Preparation time: 15–20 minutes Marinating time: 8 hours ♀♀♀

Mix the fish with the lime and lemon juice, cover, and refrigerate for at least 8 hours or overnight.

Add the remaining ingredients and leave for 1 hour at room temperature before serving.

Serves 4

1 1/2 lb (750 g) red snapper fillets, rinsed and cut into bite-sized pieces

Juice of 4 limes and 3 lemons

5 cloves garlic, chopped

1 onion, chopped fine

1 tsp (5 mL) salt

4 Tbsp (50 mL) fresh chopped cilantro

2 ripe tomatoes, diced

2 red bell peppers, diced

2 to 4 fresh medium-hot chiles such as jalapeños

1/2 tsp (2 mL) sugar

1/2 cup (125 mL) white wine vinegar, or to taste

1/4 tsp (1 mL) cumin seeds

yellow peppers *and sun-dried tomatoes*

Homemade sun-dried tomatoes are the best with this — they are tender and more flavorsome than the bottled variety, which can be tough. This appetizer, which I first tasted at a falafel stall in Tel Aviv, is delicious on small pieces of French bread or crisp crostini-like toasts.

Serves 4

3 yellow peppers, cut into bite-
   sized pieces
4–5 Tbsp (50–60 mL) extra-
   virgin olive oil
4 to 5 cloves garlic, chopped
14 oz (400 g) ripe tomatoes,
   diced (or 14-oz (398-mL) can
   tomatoes, chopped)
Pinch sugar
Salt and pepper
8 to 10 marinated sun-dried
   tomatoes, cut into quarters
1 Tbsp (15 mL) balsamic
   vinegar or to taste
2–3 tsp capers, rinsed and
   drained
Fresh chopped parsley,
   to garnish

Preparation time: 10–15 minutes Cooking time: 10–15 minutes

Brown the peppers in the olive oil for about 7 minutes, long enough to lightly brown them without them turning too soft. Add half the garlic, the diced tomatoes, sugar, salt, and pepper, and cook over high heat until the tomatoes reduce to a thick paste.

Stir in the sun-dried tomatoes, balsamic vinegar, capers, and remaining garlic, and cool to room temperature to serve. Garnish with fresh parsley if liked.

kamala's roasted red pepper
and cream cheese spread

Kamala is a colleague of mine in the food world. This flavorful appetizer is delicious spread on rustic bread or tiny boiled new potatoes. If you use roasted peppers from a bottle this takes about 5 minutes to prepare.

Preparation time: 10–15 minutes

Whirl the roasted red pepper strips in a blender or food processor to purée, then add the cream cheese and garlic and continue to purée until smooth. Season with lemon juice, salt, and pepper to taste, then mix in the oregano or marjoram. Chill until ready to serve.

Helpful hint

Enjoy a California bagel: spread the cheese mixture onto a bagel and top with layers of crisp vegetables, such as thinly sliced peppers, cucumber, red onion, and tomatoes, then close up and press tightly.

Serves 4

2 red bell peppers, roasted, peeled, and cut into strips
1 cup (250 mL) full- or low-fat cream cheese
2 to 3 cloves garlic, chopped
Lemon juice to taste
Salt
Pinch black or cayenne pepper to taste
2 tsp (10 mL) fresh chopped oregano or marjoram, or to taste

red pepper *and walnut dip*

This particular version of *Muhammarah*, a Sephardic Jewish paste of roasted red peppers and walnuts, is Syrian, rich, with a hint of heat. The original recipe calls for pomegranate molasses, but I tend to use balsamic vinegar instead, for its slight sweet-fruitiness and strong flavor.

Preparation time: 15–20 minutes

Whirl all the ingredients together either in a blender or food processor until smooth and creamy.

Serve the dip with pita bread, French bread, or spears of young Romaine lettuce.

Serves 4

3 red bell peppers, roasted, peeled, and chopped
2 to 3 mild red chiles, roasted, peeled, and chopped
1 cup (250 mL) walnut pieces
3 to 4 cloves garlic, chopped
1½ slices whole wheat bread, slightly stale, or toast
1–2 Tbsp (15–25 mL) balsamic vinegar
Juice of ½ lemon
½–1 tsp (2–5 mL) cumin
½ tsp (2 mL) sugar, or to taste
Salt to taste
⅓–½ cup (100 mL) extra-virgin olive oil

piquillo peppers *with garlic-herbed scrambled eggs*

Serves 4

2 to 3 cloves garlic, minced
Salt to taste
10 cloves garlic, sliced thin
6 Tbsp (75 mL) extra-virgin
  olive oil
6 to 8 ripe red bell peppers,
  roasted, peeled, and cut
  into strips
Bottled piquillo peppers,
  roasted and peeled
Few drops balsamic vinegar
8 eggs, lightly beaten
3–4 Tbsp (45–50 mL) milk
2 Tbsp (25 mL) butter or
  as desired
8 slices country bread
  (sourdough or ciabatta)
2 Tbsp (25 mL) fresh chopped
  parsley or cilantro

This enticing appetizer is a simplified Pipérade, with no tomatoes, onions, or ham, just the simplicity of garlic-flavored piquillo peppers, enriched with creamy, herbed scrambled eggs, and served on a slice of country bread.

Preparation time: 10–15 minutes Cooking time: 10–15 minutes

Combine the minced garlic with the salt to form a paste, or mince the whole garlic together with the salt. Set the garlic paste aside.

Meanwhile, warm the sliced garlic in a heavy skillet in the olive oil until the garlic is just turning golden then add the roasted and piquillo peppers, and a little salt, and cook, covered, for 15 to 20 minutes, or long enough for the pepper and garlic flavor to combine. Add a drop or two of balsamic vinegar, cook for a minute longer, then set aside and keep them warm.

Combine the eggs with the milk. Gently heat the butter in the skillet and when melted pour in the eggs. Cook slowly, and when half cooked add the garlic paste. Cook, stirring gently, until soft creamy curds form, but do not overcook.

Spoon some of the peppers and egg mixture onto each portion of bread, sprinkle with the parsley or cilantro, and drizzle some of the pepper juices on top. Serve immediately.

gratin *of red peppers*

Serves 4

8 red bell peppers, roasted,
  peeled, and cut into strips
⅔ cup (150 mL) heavy cream
Salt and pepper to taste
2 Tbsp (25 mL) freshly grated
  Parmesan or pecorino cheese

This gratin of red peppers in red pepper cream, from Aragon in Spain, is a rich and tempting appetizer. Serve with good bread.

Preparation time: 10–15 minutes Cooking time: 10–15 minutes

Preheat oven to 450°F (225°C).

Arrange half of the pepper strips in the bottom of a gratin dish.

Purée the remaining red peppers with the heavy cream in a blender or food processor. Season to taste.

Pour the pepper cream over the pepper strips, sprinkle with the cheese, and place briefly in the oven at 450°F (225°C) or under a hot broiler to heat through, bubble, and sizzle. Serve immediately, with bread to soak up any extra sauce.

shrimp *and hot pepper tapas*

Shrimp tapas are a treat, sizzling in their ceramic bowl, redolent

of garlic and hot peppers, and perfect for nibbling

out of their shells as you chat and drink and enjoy the evening.

Preparation time: 15–20 minutes Cooking time: 15–20 minutes

Serves 4

Combine the shrimp with half the garlic, hot pepper flakes, juice of half the lemon, and half the olive oil. Sprinkle with salt to taste; leave to marinate for at least 30 minutes. Meanwhile, cut the remaining half lemon into wedges and set aside.

Heat a skillet until very hot. Add the remaining olive oil and garlic, cook for a moment or two, then reduce the heat and add the shrimp to the skillet. Cook for a few minutes, turning occasionally, until the shrimp are opaque.

Remove the shrimp from the skillet, place on a plate and cover to keep warm, then pour in the wine and boil down until reduced to only a few spoonfuls of intensely flavored sauce, then pour it over the shrimp.

Serve hot, sprinkled with parsley and lemon wedges for squeezing over the shrimp.

1–1½ lb (500–700 g) large
  shrimp, in their shells
5 to 8 cloves garlic, chopped
Large pinch hot pepper flakes
1 lemon
5–6 Tbsp (65–75 mL) olive oil
Salt to taste
1 cup (200 mL) dry white wine
1–2 Tbsp (15–25 mL) fresh
  chopped flat leaf parsley

soups &

roasted red peppers filled *with melted cheese, prosciutto, and basil*

This simple but irresistible starter was inspired by Sri Owen, who made a similar dish combining Western and Asian flavors. She used a spicy mild red chile and scattered lots of Thai basil over the top. It was delicious.

Serves 4

4 red bell peppers, halved

2 Tbsp (25 mL) extra-virgin olive oil

3 cloves garlic, chop two, leave one whole

4 to 6 slices prosciutto, sliced thin

9 oz (250 g) Fontina or Monterey Jack, shredded

10 to 15 fresh basil leaves, sliced thin

Preparation time: 10–15 minutes Cooking time: 20–25 minutes

Preheat the oven to 425°F (220°C).

Brush the cut side of the peppers with olive oil and then rub with a whole garlic clove. Broil for approximately 5 minutes until the flesh starts to soften.

Combine the prosciutto, cheese, garlic, and basil, and divide the mixture evenly among the peppers. Arrange the cheese-stuffed peppers in a single layer in a baking pan.

Drizzle them with the olive oil, then bake for 15 to 20 minutes or long enough to melt the cheese; the peppers should just be sizzling but not browning, except in little spots.

Serve immediately, on hot plates if possible, with slices of rustic bread.

cheese and pepper *potato pancakes*

You can serve this as a bowl of soft, cheese-flavored mashed potatoes

on the first night and make any leftovers into potato pancakes.

Preparation time: 40 minutes Cooking time: 30–40 minutes

Serves 4 to 6

Cook the potatoes in salted water until they are tender; drain well and mash.

Meanwhile, sauté the onion and red and yellow pepper in the butter until the vegetables form a soft mixture, then add half the garlic and season with salt and pepper. Cook for a few minutes then remove from the heat and add to the mashed potatoes.

Beat in the Cheddar, feta, and Parmesan cheeses with the sour cream and the reserved garlic. If the mixture seems too thick and solid, thin it down with a little milk and the beaten egg.

If the mixture seems to be the right fluffy consistency do not add the liquids as the mixture will be too wet. Beat in a few tablespoons of the flour until the mixture is firm without being too hard or solid.

Take up about 2 tablespoons of the mixture, form into pancakes, and dust thoroughly with flour on both sides. Heat the oil in a large skillet or wok and when the oil is very hot, carefully add the pancakes, several at a time, and cook, turning carefully once the bottom is golden brown. Cook the other side until golden brown also, then remove from the skillet and leave to drain for a few minutes on paper towels.

Serve immediately, or allow to cool and reheat on a baking sheet for 5 to 8 minutes in the oven at 400°F (200°C).

1 lb (500 g) potatoes, peeled
  and diced
Salt and pepper
1 onion, chopped
1 each: red and yellow bell
  pepper, diced
2 Tbsp (25 mL) butter
8 cloves garlic, chopped
5 oz (150 g) Cheddar cheese,
  diced
5 oz (150 g) feta cheese,
  crumbled
¼ cup (45 mL) Parmesan
  cheese, freshly grated
2 Tbsp (25 mL) sour cream
1 egg, lightly beaten (optional)
¼–⅓ cup (45–65 mL)
  all-purpose flour, plus extra
  for dusting
Vegetable oil and olive oil
  for frying

roasted artichokes and *red peppers*
with caper mayonnaise

Hot sizzling artichokes and roasted red peppers, perfumed with garlic, and served with a sharp-tasting caper mayonnaise makes an interesting appetizer. I would follow this with a main course of roasted chicken.

Serves 4

4 artichokes or 2 large ones,
  cut in half lengthwise
2 red bell peppers, roasted,
  peeled, and cut into strips
5 cloves garlic, chopped
5 Tbsp (65 mL) extra-virgin
  olive oil
1½ Tbsp (20 mL) white wine
  vinegar
1–2 tsp (5–10 mL) fresh
  chopped oregano or marjoram
Salt and pepper to taste
2 tsp (10 mL) capers, or
  to taste
5 Tbsp (65 mL) mayonnaise

Preparation time: 20–25 minutes Cooking time: 25–45 minutes

Preheat oven to 375°F (180°C).

Precook the artichokes either by boiling, steaming, or microwaving. They should be just tender but not too soft. If boiling, drain well.

Place the artichokes in a baking pan and scatter the roasted peppers around them. Sprinkle with garlic, making sure to mix it in with the peppers and tuck some of the garlic into the artichoke leaves.

Sprinkle with the olive oil, vinegar, herbs, and salt and pepper, then bake for 15 to 20 minutes or long enough to heat through and meld the flavors together.

Meanwhile, combine the capers with the mayonnaise and chill until ready to serve. The artichokes can be served hot, warm, or at room temperature. Serve each portion of artichokes and peppers with a spoonful of caper mayonnaise.

salads

*... and more salads! Peppers are a perfect salad ingredient, crisp and raw,
chopped or sliced, stewed and eaten cold, served with or without dressing.
Here is a selection of just a few pepper salads – with peppers you can
always concoct many other flavorsome possibilities.*

mango, pepper, *and peanut salad*

Serves 4

2 Tbsp (25 mL) chopped
  peanuts or toasted sesame
  seeds
1 Tbsp (15 mL) vegetable oil
Handful arugula leaves
1 Tbsp (15 mL) extra-virgin
  olive oil
Juice of ½ lime or 1–2 tsp
  (5–10 mL) sweet rice vinegar
½ tsp (2 mL) sugar, or to taste
2 Tbsp (25 mL) orange juice
1 ripe mango, peeled and sliced
2 red bell peppers or 6 baby
  red bell peppers, thinly sliced
½ ripe mild red chile, thinly
  sliced, or drizzle chile oil
2 scallions, sliced thin
1 Tbsp (15 mL) each: fresh
  chopped cilantro and mint

This salad contains a range of flavors — sweet mango, hot chile, toasted nuts or seeds, and peppery arugula. Smoked tofu or chicken could be added if liked.

Preparation time: 10 minutes

To toast the peanuts, heat 1 tablespoon vegetable oil in a wok or skillet. When the oil just begins to smoke add the peanuts and cook over a medium-high heat for about 2 minutes until golden brown, tossing and turning as they cook. Drain on paper towels.

Arrange the arugula on a plate and dress with a mixture of the olive oil, lime juice or vinegar, sugar, and orange juice, then top with the mango, red pepper, chile, scallions, peanuts or sesame seeds, cilantro, and mint. Serve immediately.

roasted red pepper *and asparagus salad*
with parmesan and truffle oil

Serves 4

6–7 oz (175–200 g) small
  asparagus tips, trimmed
2 red bell peppers, roasted,
  peeled, and sliced into large
  julienne strips
2 cloves garlic, chopped fine
Salt to taste
2 tsp (10 mL) white wine
  vinegar
Generous drizzle truffle oil
1–1½ oz (30–40 g) Parmesan
  cheese, finely shaved

The marriage of silky roasted peppers and truffle, combined with the delicacy of asparagus and the salty tang of Parmesan cheese is an inspired one which I first tasted as a tapas in Madrid. Serve with good bread to mop up any juices.

Preparation time: 10 minutes Cooking time: 5 minutes

Blanch the asparagus in lightly salted water until brightly colored, then drain and rinse thoroughly in cold water.

Toss the peppers and asparagus in the garlic and salt, and arrange on a serving plate. Drizzle with the vinegar and truffle oil. Scatter the Parmesan shavings over the top and serve at room temperature.

mango, pepper, and peanut salad

yellow peppers *with blue cheese and basil*

Serves 4

2 to 3 yellow bell peppers, sliced

5–6 oz (150–175 g) blue cheese such as Gorgonzola or Roquefort, crumbled or diced

1–2 tsp (5–10 mL) balsamic vinegar or white wine vinegar

1–2 Tbsp (15–25 mL) extra-virgin olive oil

5–6 Tbsp (65–75 mL) fresh basil leaves, torn

Blue-veined cheese, yellow peppers, and fresh green basil leaves:

this simple salad is as beautiful to look at as it is refreshing.

Preparation time: 5–10 minutes

Arrange the peppers on a plate and scatter the blue cheese over the top. Drizzle with balsamic or wine vinegar, then with olive oil, and sprinkle over the shredded basil. Serve immediately.

spicy crab *salad*

Serves 4

3 shallots or ¼ red onion, chopped fine

1 fresh chile, such as jalapeño or serrano, chopped

Juice of ½ lime

1 Tbsp (15 mL) white wine or fruit vinegar

1 tsp (5 mL) fresh chopped marjoram or ½ tsp (0.5 mL) fresh chopped oregano

1 tsp (5 mL) fresh chopped cilantro

1 Tbsp (15 mL) olive oil

8–12 oz (240–360 g) cooked crab meat

1 avocado, peeled and sliced

Radishes, thinly sliced

In the Yucatan, where temperatures soar to almost unbearable heights,

you will find salady dishes called *fiambre* – cool mixtures of hot

spicy ingredients. Often these *fiambres* are rolled up in tender fresh

tortillas for hot-weather tacos.

Preparation time: 10 minutes (using cooked crab meat)

Combine the shallots or onion with the chile, lime juice, vinegar, marjoram or oregano, cilantro, and olive oil. Mix lightly with the crab.
  Serve garnished with the avocado and radishes.

north african red *and green pepper salad*
with cucumbers and olives

A perfect day: go to the market and fill your bag with the crispest of cucumbers and peppers, juicy tomatoes, salty black olives, and fine hot chiles, then take it all home and arrange it on a platter with fragrant herbs, douse it with some good olive oil, and serve for lunch.

Preparation time: 15 minutes 🌶🌶🌶

Combine the cucumbers with the peppers, garlic, salt, and chile or cayenne pepper, and toss well. Arrange in a bowl and mix with the olives, then toss with the olive oil and vinegar.

Chill until ready to serve, and toss with the cilantro and mint before serving.

Serves 4

1 large or 2 small cucumbers, peeled and sliced thin

1 each: red and green bell pepper, sliced thin

3 to 4 garlic cloves, chopped

Salt to taste

½ to 1 fresh hot chile, chopped, or cayenne pepper to taste

1 cup (250 mL) olives, pitted and halved

4–5 Tbsp (50–65 mL) extra-virgin olive oil

1–1½ Tbsp (15–20 mL) white wine vinegar, or to taste

1½ Tbsp (20 mL) each: fresh chopped cilantro and mint

spanish salad *of frisée*

This salad is simple to prepare, and deeply refreshing when the weather is hot: frisée, with its refreshing, slightly-bitter flavor; the peppers with their distinctive Mediterranean flavor; and the olives and blue cheese, with their pungent, salty bite.

Preparation time: 15 minutes

Arrange the frisée, and garnish with the roasted bell peppers, blue cheese, and green olives. Dress with olive oil, sherry vinegar, and tomato vinaigrette. Serve immediately.

Serves 4

1 small head of frisée, cleaned and cored, cut into bite-sized pieces (use another bitter lettuce variety if unavailable)

2 red bell peppers, roasted, peeled, and cut into strips

3 oz (100 g) ripe Spanish cabrales, a blue cheese

10–15 pimiento-stuffed green olives

3 Tbsp (45 mL) extra-virgin olive oil

1 Tbsp (15 mL) sherry vinegar

2 Tbsp (25 mL) tomato vinaigrette

turkish white beans in *chile-tomato dressing*
with green pepper

Serves 4

1¹⁄₂ lb (750 g) ripe tomatoes, diced (or 14-oz (398-mL) can tomatoes, chopped)
Salt to taste
Pinch sugar
1 small to medium-sized onion, chopped fine
1 medium to medium-hot fresh red chile, chopped fine
¹⁄₂ to 1 red bell pepper, chopped
3 cloves garlic, chopped
Juice and zest of ¹⁄₂ to 1 lemon
3–4 Tbsp (45–50 mL) extra-virgin olive oil
14-oz (398-mL) can white beans, drained
1 green bell pepper, sliced thin

The combination of tender white beans in a spicy tomato and chile sauce is a satisfying one, especially with the addition of crisp green pepper.

Preparation time: 10 minutes Cooking time: 10–15 minutes

Place the tomatoes in a small saucepan, preferably nonstick, and cook over medium heat, stirring occasionally with a wooden spoon, until the tomatoes reduce in volume to about 5–6 tablespoons. Season with salt and sugar and leave to cool.

Combine with the onion, chile, pepper, garlic, lemon juice and zest, olive oil, beans, and green pepper. Chill until ready to serve.

italian fennel and pepper salad
with black olives

Serves 4

1 medium to large or 2 small to medium bulbs fennel, trimmed and sliced thin
Juice of ¹⁄₂ to 1 lemon
2 red bell peppers, sliced thin
1 cup (250 mL) black olives in oil
3–4 Tbsp (45–50 mL) extra-virgin olive oil
Sprinkling of fresh herbs such as marjoram (optional)

I assembled this simple salad one day on an Italian beach after visiting the little morning market in a village in the area of the Cinque Terre. We bought sardines off a boat, made a fire to cook them on, and savored one of the most perfect meals of my life.

Preparation time: 10–15 minutes

Toss the fennel with a few drops of the lemon juice to prevent discoloration. Arrange the fennel and the red peppers on a plate. Garnish with the black olives and drizzle with the olive oil and lemon juice to taste. Sprinkle with a little chopped fresh herbs if wished.

thai vegetable salad *with red pepper dressing*

This is a spicy Pacific Rim coleslaw, full of invigorating vegetable

flavors with a dressing of roasted sweet peppers spiced with hot pepper flakes.

It is delicious with a sandwich, or as part of a summer buffet or picnic.

Preparation time: 15–20 minutes

Cook the squash or corn on the cob until just tender; if using squash leave it to cool. If using corn on the cob cut it off the cobs. Set the vegetable aside.

Chop the roasted peppers and combine them in a food processor with the garlic, hot pepper flakes, chile, soy or fish sauce, balsamic vinegar, sugar, and lime juice. Process until the mixture becomes a thick chunky paste.

Combine the onion and cabbage with the squash or corn, the basil, cilantro, and mint. Toss with the red pepper dressing, and adjust the seasoning to taste.

Chill until ready to eat.

Serves 4

1 to 2 golden squash or yellow crookneck squash, or 1 to 2 ears corn on the cob

2 red bell peppers, roasted and peeled (or use bottled peppers)

5 cloves garlic, chopped

½ tsp (2 mL) hot pepper flakes (or more), to taste

½ fresh chile, or more to taste, chopped (optional)

1 Tbsp (15 mL) light soy sauce or fish sauce

1 Tbsp (15 mL) balsamic vinegar, or to taste

3–4 Tbsp (45–50 mL) sugar

Juice of ½ lime, or more to taste

5–6 Tbsp (65–75 mL) red onion, chopped, or scallions, sliced thin

½ medium to large white cabbage, shredded

3–4 Tbsp (45–50 mL) each: fresh chopped basil, cilantro, and mint

turkish roasted pepper *and peach salad*

Serves 4

2 each: green and red bell
peppers
3 ripe peaches or nectarines
3 green onions or ½ red onion,
chopped
2 to 3 cloves garlic,
chopped fine
2 Tbsp (25 mL) extra-virgin
olive oil
2–3 tsp (10–15 mL) balsamic
vinegar
Juice of ½ lemon, or to taste
1½ tsp (7 mL) sugar, or to taste
Generous pinch paprika
and cayenne pepper
2–3 Tbsp (25–45 mL) fresh
chopped mint
1–2 tsp (5–10 mL) fresh
chopped dill or tarragon
(optional)

A deliciously refreshing salad to serve on a scorching day, this
Turkish salad can be served as a first course or as part of a selection of salads.
A cold roasted chicken would make this a perfect summer picnic lunch.

Preparation time: 5–10 minutes

Roast the peppers over an open flame until they char, then peel. Remove the stem and slice the flesh into wide strips. Cut the peaches or nectarines into pieces about the same size, and add this to the peppers, then mix in the onion, garlic, olive oil, vinegar, lemon juice, sugar, paprika, and cayenne pepper. Finally mix in the herbs, then serve immediately or chill until ready to serve.

eggplant *and roasted red peppers*

Serves 4

1 medium to large eggplant,
sliced crosswise
Salt to taste
5–6 Tbsp (65–75 mL) extra-
virgin olive oil
1–2 Tbsp (15–25 mL) white
wine vinegar
5 cloves garlic, chopped
2 red bell peppers, roasted,
peeled, and thinly sliced
Black pepper to taste
3–4 Tbsp (45–50 mL) fresh
chopped flat leaf parsley

Broiled eggplant slices are tossed with roasted red peppers and a
garlicky vinaigrette, then left to marinate. Serve at room
temperature. This also makes a wonderful sandwich filling, layered
with sliced mozzarella and served in focaccia or a roll.

Preparation time: 15 minutes Cooking time: 15–20

To degorge the eggplant, sprinkle generously with salt and leave for 30 minutes or until brown droplets of juice appear. Rinse the eggplant well and pat dry.
If you prefer not to degorge the eggplant, simply salt as you would any vegetable.
Brush the eggplant slices with olive oil and broil on both sides until they are lightly browned; alternatively you can fry them or cook them on a barbecue.
Layer the hot eggplant slices, sprinkling with the remaining olive oil, vinegar, garlic, peppers, black pepper, and parsley. Serve at room temperature, or chill until ready to serve.

turkish roasted pepper and peach salad

israeli breakfast salad

In Israel, breakfast is salad. Most meals in Israel include salad: crisp, crunchy, and juicy with a wide variety of ingredients, which always include green, yellow, and red peppers, and hot peppers too if you wish.

Serves 4 to 6

1 cucumber, unpeeled and diced

1 each: green, red, yellow or orange bell pepper, diced

6 ripe tomatoes, diced

2 Tbsp (25 mL) each: fresh chopped parsley, cilantro, dill (optional), and mint (optional)

3 cloves garlic, chopped

3 scallions, sliced thin

Salt to taste

$\frac{1}{2}$ to 1 hot chile, chopped (optional)

3–4 Tbsp (45–50 mL) extra-virgin olive oil

Juice of 1 to 1$\frac{1}{2}$ lemons

Preparation time: 10–15 minutes

Combine all the ingredients and chill until ready to serve.

cabbage and green pepper salad
with cucumber and feta cheese

This simple salad is typical of the many variations on the classic Greek salad.

It is a crisp, cool, and refreshing hot-weather dish.

Preparation time: 10 minutes

Arrange the cabbage on a plate and top with the green pepper, then sprinkle with the cucumber and garnish with the feta cheese.

Drizzle the olive oil and vinegar (or vinegar and lemon juice) over the salad as a dressing, and sprinkle with oregano. Serve immediately, or chill until ready to serve.

Serves 4

½ white or green cabbage, sliced very thin

1 green bell pepper, sliced very thin

½ cucumber, diced

4 oz (125 g) feta cheese, cut into bite-sized pieces

4 Tbsp (50 mL) extra-virgin olive oil

1 Tbsp (25 mL) white wine vinegar (or half wine vinegar and half lemon juice)

Several pinches oregano

sweet potato, tomato, *and*
roasted red pepper salad

Bright orange sweet potatoes, scarlet red roasted peppers, and tomatoes make

this a vivid appetizer. It is also delicious picnic food.

Preparation time: 10 minutes
Cooking time: 1 hour if conventional oven or stovetop, 5 minutes if microwave

Cook the sweet potatoes by steaming, boiling, or in the microwave until tender. Allow to cool, then cut them into bite-sized chunks.

Arrange the roasted peppers, sweet potatoes, and tomatoes together on a plate, then sprinkle with the garlic, salt, cayenne, and sugar then the vinegar and olive oil. Taste for seasoning and either serve immediately, or chill until ready to serve.

Serves 4

2 small to medium-sized orange-fleshed sweet potatoes, unpeeled

2 red bell peppers, roasted, peeled, and cut into bite-sized pieces (bottled peppers can be used)

2 to 3 small, flavorful tomatoes, diced

3 cloves garlic, chopped

Salt, cayenne, and pinch sugar, to taste

1 Tbsp (15 mL) white wine vinegar

2 Tbsp (25 mL) extra-virgin olive oil

moroccan carrot *and red pepper salad*

Serves 4

2 large carrots, peeled and
  cut into 2 to 3 parts
Salt
Pinch sugar
½ red bell pepper, sliced thin
¼ fresh red chile, chopped
Pinch cumin
Juice of ½ lemon, or to taste
1 Tbsp (15 mL) olive oil
  (optional)

The flavor of the carrots in this simple but delicious salad is enhanced by cooking them first, then shredding them rather than the other way round.

Preparation time: 10 minutes Cooking time: 10 minutes

Cook the carrots in rapidly boiling slightly salted water with a pinch of sugar. Cook until the carrots are half-tender; remove from the heat and allow to cool a little.

Shred the carrots onto a plate and sprinkle with salt and a little sugar, then toss with the red pepper, chile, and cumin.

Arrange on a plate, drizzle with lemon juice and olive oil, and serve at cool room temperature.

garbanzos in *red pepper vinaigrette*

Serves 4

5 cloves garlic, chopped
1 red bell pepper, roasted,
  peeled, and chopped
3 ripe tomatoes, chopped
1 onion, chopped
2 tsp (10 mL) paprika
Salt and pepper
2–3 tsp (10–15 mL) fresh or
  dried mixed herbs: oregano,
  rosemary, thyme, herbes de
  Provence
4–5 Tbsp (50–65 mL) white or
  red wine vinegar
4–5 Tbsp (50–65 mL) extra-
  virgin olive oil
1 lb (500 g) cooked, drained
  garbanzos (chickpeas) or
  (2 x 14-oz (398-mL) cans
  garbanzos, drained)
½ each: red and green bell
  pepper, diced
¼ to ½ fresh chile, chopped, or
  cayenne pepper to taste
  (optional)
Pinch sugar (optional)
1 Tbsp (15 mL) fresh chopped
  parsley or cilantro

This makes a superb accompaniment to most barbecued dishes,

as well as a salad tapas.

Preparation time: 15 minutes

Combine the garlic, roasted red pepper, tomatoes, onion, paprika, salt and pepper, herbs, and vinegar and mix well.

Add the olive oil, garbanzos, diced red and green peppers, chile, and sugar if necessary; taste for seasoning.

Chill until ready to serve, then sprinkle with parsley or cilantro.

mixed peppers stewed *with tomatoes and garlic*

Peperonata is a versatile Italian dish which can be served as an antipasto, with other salads and vegetables, with bread and goat cheese as an appetizer, or as a side salad with almost any buffet meal. It also makes excellent picnic fare, and can even be tossed with cold rice or pasta for a flavorful salad.

Preparation time: 10 minutes Cooking time: 1 hour

Preheat the oven to 400°F (200°C).

Place the peppers in a single layer in a shallow baking pan. Toss them with the garlic then with the olive oil, vinegar, oregano, salt, and sugar.

Bake for about 40 minutes, turning once or twice. Remove from the oven, taste, and add more vinegar, salt, and sugar if necessary. Return to the oven for a further 5 to 10 minutes.

Remove from the oven and sprinkle with the parsley or basil. Serve hot, warm, or at cool room temperature.

Serves 4 to 6

2 each: red, green, yellow bell
    pepper, cut into small pieces
6 cloves garlic, chopped
5–6 Tbsp (65–75 mL) extra-
    virgin olive oil
1–2 Tbsp (15–25 mL) red wine
    vinegar
1 Tbsp (15 mL) fresh chopped
    oregano
Salt to taste
1/4–1/2 tsp (1–2 mL) sugar
1 Tbsp (15 mL) fresh chopped
    parsley or 2 Tbsp (25 mL)
    fresh chopped basil

This peperonata has been topped with goat cheese.

rice and roasted *pepper salad*

Throughout the south of France, especially in the area around Nice, leftover rice is dressed with vinaigrette and tossed with fresh vegetables such as peppers, olives, and herbs. My rice salad tends to be on the sharp side: if you prefer a milder flavor, reduce the amount of vinegar and mustard.

Serves 4

1 cup (250 mL) rice, preferably long-grain
4 to 5 cloves garlic, chopped
¼ onion, chopped
1 medium bottle green pimiento-stuffed olives, halved
1 red bell pepper, roasted, peeled, and chopped (a bottled pepper is fine)
1 to 3 mild to medium green chiles, roasted, peeled, and chopped
½–1 tsp (2–5 mL) French mustard, preferably Dijon
Generous pinch each: turmeric and curry powder
1 Tbsp (15 mL) mixed fresh herbs: sage, mint, cilantro, and oregano, or to taste
Salt and black pepper
Dash of Tabasco or hot sauce
1 ripe tomato, diced, including the juices
3–4 Tbsp (45–50 mL) extra-virgin olive oil
1 Tbsp (15 mL) white wine vinegar
1 tsp (5 mL) balsamic vinegar
1 Tbsp (15 mL) fresh chopped parsley

Preparation time: 20 minutes Cooking time: 10 minutes

Cook the rice in 1 cup (250 ml) water until it is al dente, then fork to separate. If using freshly made rice add the rest of the ingredients and leave to cool. Taste for seasoning before serving and freshen up the flavors to taste.

sweet-sour cabbage *and pepper slaw*

Coleslaw can be delicious: shredded fresh cabbage and other vegetables with a light tangy-sweet dressing. Red and green peppers add their distinctive flavor to this coleslaw.

Preparation time: 15 minutes

Combine all the ingredients, mix well, and chill until ready to serve. Drain off excess liquid before serving.

Serves 4

½ white or green cabbage, shredded
½ onion, sliced thin
1 each: red and green bell pepper, sliced very thin
4 Tbsp (50 mL) sugar
3–4 Tbsp (45–50 mL) cider vinegar
3–4 Tbsp (45–50 mL) yogurt
1–2 Tbsp (15–25 mL) mayonnaise
Salt and pepper to taste
¼ tsp (1 mL) caraway seeds

roasted pepper salad *with sun-dried tomatoes and goat cheese*

This salad is like having everything that is good about the Mediterranean on your plate. Inspired by a lunch prepared by food writer and novelist Leslie Forbes, it also makes a suitable appetizer for a dinner that is either Mediterranean in flavor, or veers into the Indian Subcontinent.

Preparation time: 20 minutes

In a heavy ungreased skillet lightly roast the almond slivers over medium-low heat, turning them occasionally until lightly browned and fragrant. Do not burn. Allow to cool.

Arrange the frisée lettuce on a platter, then arrange the peppers around the leaves, and the sun-dried tomatoes and cheese around these. Scatter the roasted almonds over the salad, along with the basil and garlic, then drizzle with olive oil and vinegar. Serve immediately.

Serves 4

1 cup (250 mL) slivered almonds
Handful bitter salad leaves, such as frisée
2 to 3 each: red and yellow bell peppers, roasted, peeled, and sliced
12 to 15 marinated sun-dried tomatoes, chopped
5 oz (150 g) goat cheese, crumbled or chopped
Handful fresh basil, sliced thin
3 cloves garlic, or to taste
4 Tbsp (50 mL) extra-virgin olive oil, or as desired
1 Tbsp (15 mL) white wine vinegar (or half sherry vinegar, half balsamic vinegar), or to taste

salt cod salad

Serves 4

14 oz (400 g) dried salt cod,
broken into several pieces

4 to 6 scallions, minced

¹/₂ to 1 fresh red chile, chopped

¹/₃–¹/₂ cup (100 mL) extra-virgin
olive oil

3 Tbsp (45 mL) sherry vinegar

Handful black peppercorns,
crushed, to taste

2 to 3 ripe flavorful tomatoes,
diced

1 each: red and green bell
pepper, sliced thin

2–3 oz (75 g) black olives in oil

Serve *Exqueixada*, this Spanish salad of dried salt cod, richly flavored with peppers, tomatoes, onions, and sherry vinegar, for lunch, or as a first course followed by a barbecue of vegetables, lamb, or fish, with perhaps a bowl of Red Pepper Aïoli (p. 136).

Preparation time: 15 minutes Standing time: 3 hours and 1¹/₂ days

Place the salt cod in a bowl and cover with water. Refrigerate and leave for 3 hours, drain well, and cover with water again. Leave for about 1¹/₂ days. Drain and squeeze out the excess moisture.

Using your fingers, tear the flesh of the cod into shreds, discarding the skin and bones; alternatively slice the flesh diagonally, in slivers (also discarding the skin and bones).

Mix the onion, chile, olive oil, vinegar, crushed peppercorns, and shredded fish in a shallow bowl and leave for about 30 minutes. When ready to serve garnish the platter with the tomatoes, peppers, and olives.

seafood and red pepper *salad with*
tarragon aïoli

Serves 4

14 oz (400 g) cooked seafood

2–3 Tbsp (25–45 mL) Pernod, or
to taste, or 2 Tbsp (25 mL) of
fresh chopped fennel leaves

Juice of ¹/₂ to 1 lemon

Salt and pepper to taste

2 red bell peppers, roasted,
peeled, and chopped

1 very ripe tomato, diced

4 to 6 cloves garlic, chopped fine

¹/₂–³/₄ cup (125–175 mL)
mayonnaise

3–4 Tbsp (45–50 mL) extra-
virgin olive oil

2 tsp (10 mL) fresh chopped
tarragon

Handful of mixed salad leaves,
dressed with a small amount of
olive oil and vinegar or lemon

A seafood selection including crab, lobster, and shrimp, combined with flavorful roasted red peppers and served with a creamy aïoli spiked with tarragon, makes perfect picnic fare or an alfresco lunch for a hot day.

Preparation time: 20 minutes

Toss the seafood with Pernod or fennel leaves, lemon juice, salt and pepper, then with the chopped red peppers and tomato. Set aside.

Combine the garlic with the mayonnaise, then stir in the olive oil and tarragon and taste for seasoning.

Make a bed or mound of the salad leaves on a platter and arrange the seafood on top. Garnish it with a spoonful of the tarragon aïoli and the remaining red peppers.

Helpful hint

If seafood is unavailable, this salad can also be prepared with shredded, poached chicken.

mediterranean chicken, *asparagus,*
and pepper salad with black olive aïoli

This salad combines my favorite ingredients — chicken, black olives, roasted peppers, asparagus, and crisp salad leaves. This salad is also a delicious sandwich filling for French bread or a good-quality focaccia.

Preparation time: 15 minutes (using already cooked chicken)

Preheat oven to 400°F (200°C).

To roast the asparagus, toss lightly in 1–2 teaspoons of the olive oil and salt and pepper to taste. Place asparagus in a single layer on a baking sheet and cook in oven for 8–10 minutes, turning once or twice until it is lightly browned in spots, crunchy yet tender.

Toss the salad leaves with about two-thirds of the olive oil and the balsamic vinegar. Arrange on a platter or individual serving plates, and top with the cooled asparagus, roasted pepper strips, and chicken.

Mix the black olive aïoli: combine the mayonnaise with the garlic and tapénade, and whisk in the remaining olive oil. Season with the lemon juice to taste. If the mixture curdles, add a little more mayonnaise.

Garnish the salad with a spoonful of black olive aïoli and sprinkle with basil. Serve immediately.

Serves 4

5 asparagus spears (125 g), trimmed
3–4 Tbsp (45–50 mL) extra-virgin olive oil
Salt and pepper, to taste
7 oz (200 g) mixed salad leaves
1 tsp (15 mL) balsamic vinegar, or to taste
1 each: red and yellow bell peppers, roasted, peeled, and cut into large strips
1 small roasted chicken, the meat skinned and cut into bite-sized pieces
½ cup (75 mL) mayonnaise
2 cloves garlic, chopped
1–2 Tbsp (15–25 mL) tapénade
Juice of ¼ lemon
Handful fresh basil leaves, torn

coronation chicken *with red peppers, seedless raisins, and cashew nuts*

Serves 4 to 6

1 small to medium-sized
  chicken (about 2 lb/1 kg),
  roasted or poached, the meat
  cut off the bone and chopped
  into bite-sized pieces
3 cloves garlic, chopped
3 scallions, sliced thin
2 red bell peppers, diced
½–1 tsp (2–5 mL) curry powder
¼–½ tsp (1–2 mL) cumin,
  or to taste
½–⅔ cup (75–100 mL)
  mayonnaise
½–⅔ cup (75–100 mL) yogurt
6 Tbsp (75 mL) seedless raisins
⅓–½ cup (65–75 mL) chopped
  cashew nuts, toasted
Salt and pepper to taste
3–4 Tbsp (45–50 mL) fresh
  chopped cilantro and/or mint

Coronation chicken, a dish devised for Queen Elizabeth II's coronation, has become a firm favorite. There are many versions, all equally delicious.

It is a perfect lunch salad, or an appetizer to precede a big soup supper.

Preparation time: 15 minutes (using cooked chicken)

Combine the diced chicken with the remaining ingredients except for the herbs. Taste for seasoning and adjust the quantity of mayonnaise and yogurt to achieve the desired consistency.

Chill until ready to serve, garnished with the cilantro and/or mint.

poultry, meat, & fish

Many traditional main courses of poultry, meat, and fish can be enlivened with the addition of peppers. With so many cuisines to choose from, and so many peppers to add their color and flavor, it wasn't easy to limit myself to the following selection.

pacific rim chicken *with cashew nuts, peppers, and hoisin sauce*

Hoison sauce gives this stir-fry an authentic Chinese flavor. Hoisin sauce and 5-spice powder are available at all Chinese grocers and most large supermarkets.

A stir-fry should be cooked when virtually everything else for your meal is ready.

As a fiery touch, I often sprinkle this dish with a chopped jalapeño.

Serves 4

2 chicken breasts, skinned
   and boned, cut into
   bite-sized pieces
1 Tbsp (15 mL) sugar, or to
   taste
Salt
1 tsp (5 mL) soy sauce, to taste
1 tsp (5 mL) sherry or rice wine
1 Tbsp (15 mL) cornstarch
1 onion, cut into bite-sized
   pieces
4–5 Tbsp (50–65 mL) vegetable
   oil, or as needed
3 cloves garlic, chopped
2 tsp (10 mL) chopped ginger
   root
1 each: red and green bell
   pepper, cut into bite-sized
   pieces
15 water chestnuts (canned is
   fine) cut into quarters
1/3–1/2 cup (65–75 mL)
   hoisin sauce
Large pinch Chinese 5-spice
   powder
1 cup (250 mL) chicken broth
5–6 Tbsp (65–75 mL) water
2 tsp (10 mL) sesame oil, or to
   taste
3 scallions, sliced thin
3 Tbsp (45 mL) each: fresh
   chopped cilantro and mint
1 cup (250 mL) cashew nuts

Preparation time: 15–20 minutes Cooking time: 5–10 minutes

Combine the chicken with 1/2 teaspoon of the sugar, a pinch of salt, 1 teaspoon soy sauce, the sherry or rice wine, and the cornstarch. Mix well and set aside.

   In a wok, stir-fry the onion in a tablespoon or so of the oil (if you don't have a wok, a large, well-seasoned cast-iron pan can be used instead), then add the garlic and ginger and cook for a few minutes. Remove from the wok and add another tablespoon of the oil. Stir-fry the red and green peppers and the water chestnuts, then remove from the wok.

   Add the remaining oil and stir-fry the chicken, cooking it with its marinade until the chicken is just opaque, 3 to 4 minutes. Remove from the wok.

   Add the hoisin sauce, 5-spice powder, chicken broth, remaining sugar, and water and heat through then return the vegetables and chicken to the wok and mix together for a few moments. Turn onto a plate and drizzle with sesame oil, then sprinkle generously with scallions, cilantro, mint, and cashew nuts. Serve immediately.

Vegetarian Variation

   Use tofu to replace the chicken. Fry the tofu in a wok first, until the tofu is crisp on the outside and tender inside. Drain on paper towels, and proceed as above.

pacific rim chicken with cashew nuts, peppers, and hoisin sauce

moroccan chicken *with garbanzos and mixed peppers*

Strands of red, green, and yellow peppers make this chicken tajine as attractive as it is delicious. Serve with flatbread.

Serves 4

2 lb (1 kg) chicken thighs, skinned

Salt to taste

5 cloves garlic, chopped

1 onion, sliced thin

3 Tbsp (45 mL) extra-virgin olive oil

1 tsp cumin seeds

½ tsp (2 mL) turmeric, or more to taste

½ tsp (2 mL) paprika

5 cardamom pods

¼ tsp (1 mL) ground ginger, or more to taste

½ tsp (2 mL) mild Madras curry powder, or more to taste

¼ fresh green or red chile, or more to taste, chopped

¾–1 cup (175–250 mL) chicken broth

1 each: red, yellow, green bell pepper, roasted, peeled, and sliced

14-oz (398-mL) can garbanzos (chickpeas), drained

2 lemons

¼–⅓ cup (45–65 mL) fresh chopped cilantro

Preparation time: 15 minutes Cooking time: 20 minutes

Toss the chicken thighs with the salt and garlic and set aside while you prepare the remaining ingredients.

Lightly sauté the onion in the extra-virgin olive oil until it softens, then sprinkle in the cumin seeds and allow them to roast, over medium low heat. Sprinkle in the remaining spices: turmeric, paprika, cardamom, ginger, curry powder, and the chile, and stir for a few minutes to release their fragrance.

Add the chicken thighs, and cook briefly on each side, until golden with the onion-spice mixture.

Add the broth, roasted red, yellow, and green peppers, and garbanzos, and continue to cook, stirring occasionally, for 15 to 20 minutes or until the chicken is done.

Cut one of the lemons in half and squeeze it over the chicken. Sprinkle with cilantro and serve with the remaining lemon cut into wedges.

chicken paillard *with red pepper sauce*

Chicken breasts, pounded flat, sautéed in butter, and served with a pepper sauce, this is a luxurious dish which is both simple and relatively inexpensive.

Preparation time: 15–20 minutes Cooking time: 20–30 minutes

In 2 tablespoons butter gently sauté the shallots, garlic, and peppers for a few minutes, until the shallots are soft. Add the tomatoes and cook for a few minutes longer until the mixture forms a saucelike consistency. Sprinkle in half the flour and cook, stirring, for a few minutes longer.

Stir in the broth and wine, and cook until the sauce thickens. Don't worry about any lumps because the sauce will be puréed.

Purée the sauce in a blender or food processor, or use a handheld blender. Transfer to a saucepan, stir in the cream, and warm through together; taste for salt and pepper and season to taste. Remove from heat and set aside.

Pound the chicken breasts lightly until they are even in thickness. Dust with the remaining flour and sauté the chicken breasts in the remaining butter, adding more if needed. Season with salt and pepper to taste.

Gently reheat the sauce and serve on warmed plates topped with the sautéed chicken breasts. Garnish with the fresh herbs and serve immediately.

Serves 4 to 6

6 Tbsp (75 mL) butter
3 to 5 shallots, chopped
3 to 5 cloves garlic, chopped
3 red bell peppers, roasted, peeled, and sliced
2 to 3 ripe tomatoes, chopped
4–5 Tbsp (50–65 mL) all-purpose flour, or as needed
$\frac{1}{2}$ cup (125 mL) chicken broth
$\frac{1}{2}$ cup (125 mL) dry white wine
$\frac{1}{2}$ cup (125 mL) heavy cream
6 chicken breasts, skinned and boned
Salt and pepper
3 Tbsp (45 mL) fresh basil or marjoram to garnish

tarragon chicken *with red peppers and garlic*

A simple, appealing dish. I like to insert a few sprigs of tarragon and some garlic under the skin of the chicken, for a stronger flavor.

Preparation time: 10 minutes Cooking time: 20–30 minutes

Loosen the skin of the chicken and insert a small handful of tarragon sprigs and chopped garlic underneath, between the meat and the skin. Season with salt and pepper and squeeze of lemon juice. Pat the skin back into position. Pat the chicken dry with paper towels, then sprinkle with salt and pepper on the outside.

Preheat oven to 325°F (160°C). Heat half the olive oil in a heavy skillet and brown the chicken fairly evenly; remove from the pan and place in a ceramic roasting pan. Pour off the fat from the skillet and add the peppers and sliced garlic, then the chicken broth. Stir for a few minutes, then pour into the pan with the chicken.

Drizzle the remaining olive oil over the chicken and peppers, and place in the oven to cook for about 30 minutes for leg or thigh portions or 15 to 20 minutes for breast portions.

Remove from the oven, spoon off any excess fat from the sauce, then squeeze the remaining lemon over the top of the chicken, and serve garnished with the rest of the fresh tarragon.

Serves 4

4 chicken quarters
Handful fresh tarragon sprigs
10 cloves garlic, half chopped, half sliced
Salt and pepper to taste
Juice of $\frac{1}{2}$ lemon
6 Tbsp (75 mL) extra-virgin olive oil
2 red bell peppers, roasted, peeled, and sliced
$\frac{1}{2}$ cup (125 mL) chicken broth

duck tikka kebobs *with peppers*

Served with a selection of other dishes, this will stretch to feed eight.

Duck is a delicious meat to marinate, skewer, and broil. The breast meat is

dark and flavorful, and any potential toughness is not a problem, because

marinade tenderizes the meat. This is also quite a lean way to enjoy duck.

Serves 4 to 6

4 duck breasts, about 1 lb (500 g) in total

8 cloves garlic, chopped

½ tsp (2 mL) salt

1–1½ tsp (5–7 mL) balsamic vinegar

3 Tbsp (45 mL) olive oil

1 piece sun-dried red pepper, sliced (optional)

3 Tbsp (45 mL) yogurt

3 Tbsp (45 mL) tomato paste

1 onion, minced

1 Tbsp (15 mL) tamarind paste

1 Tbsp (15 mL) paprika

1 tsp (5 mL) dried ginger

1 Tbsp (15 mL) chopped ginger root

1 tsp (5 mL) cumin

¼ tsp (1 mL) fresh coriander

Large pinch nutmeg

½ hot chile, chopped, or several dashes hot sauce

1 each: yellow, red, green, orange bell peppers, cut into bite-sized pieces

Preparation time: 15–20 minutes
Marinating time: 2 hours–2 days Cooking time: 10–15 minutes

Remove the skin from the duck breasts. Take one of the skins and cut into small pieces to thread onto the skewers with the duck to keep it moist. You can save the remaining skins for another use, such as rendering into flavorful duck fat. Keep in the freezer until needed.

Cut the duck breasts into large bite-sized pieces. Mix together half the garlic, salt, the balsamic vinegar, olive oil, and sun-dried red pepper if using, and toss the duck pieces in the mixture. Marinate for 1 hour, then add the yogurt, tomato paste, onion, tamarind paste, paprika, dried ginger, chopped ginger root, cumin, coriander, nutmeg, hot chile or sauce, remaining garlic, and salt. Cover well and leave overnight in the refrigerator, or at room temperature for about 2 hours.

Thread onto metal skewers (or use bamboo skewers which you have soaked for 30 minutes in cold water) with alternating pieces of different colored peppers and some of the small pieces of skin. Brush with melted butter if liked.

Cook the duck kebobs on the barbecue or under the broiler until lightly browned on the outside and tender inside, only about 3 to 5 minutes per side.
Serve immediately.

Helpful hint

Serve duck tikka as you would any tandoor dish: with a raita, a spiced chutney, a naan flatbread or rice, and stir-fried spiced vegetables.

duck tikka kebobs with peppers

chile-braised beef, *new mexican style*

Tender beef and red peppers are braised together in this New Mexican pot roast. Enjoy shreds of the meat and peppers wrapped up in soft flour tortillas, with diced avocado, salsa, and sour cream on the side.

Serves 4 to 6

4 to 5 mild chiles such as New Mexico, pasilla, or California

1 each: green and red bell pepper, sliced

4 ripe tomatoes, diced

1 small to medium bunch fresh cilantro, chopped

5 cloves garlic, chopped

1 onion, chopped

2 fresh bay leaves

1½ tsp (7 mL) cumin

Salt to taste

2–3 lb (1–1½ kg) beef such as chuck or other cut suitable for braising

1 cup (250 mL) beef broth

1 cup (250 mL) beer

Preparation time: 10–15 minutes Cooking time: about 3 hours

Lightly toast the chiles over an open flame then place them in a bowl. Add hot water to cover and allow to soak for at least an hour. Remove from the water, discard the stems and seeds, and either purée the chiles with some of the liquid, then strain away the tough bits of fiber, or scrape the flesh from the chiles. Discard the skin and reserve the flesh or puréed chile mixture.

Preheat oven to 350°F (190°C). Place half of the remaining peppers, vegetables, seasonings, and spices in the bottom of a baking pan, along with half the reserved chile mixture. Top with the meat, then top with the other half of the ingredients. Add the broth and beer. Cover tightly with foil.

Bake for 2 to 3 hours or until the beef is very tender, adding more liquid if needed to keep the meat from burning. Remove the foil and bake for a further 30 minutes, increasing the heat if necessary to brown and crisp the top. Serve hot.

cuban beef *with peppers and spices*

This hearty Cuban dish, known as *Vaca Frita*, is cooked shredded beef, marinated in lime juice and spices, crisply fried in olive oil and then tossed with olive oil-browned onions, lots of chopped sweet peppers, and a spoonful or two of fresh salsa to offset the richness.

Preparation time: 30 minutes Cooking time: 2–2½ hours

Serves 6

Place the meat in a pot with one of the onions, the carrot, and about a third of the garlic. Add the bouillon cubes, salt, and enough water to cover the meat. Bring to a boil then simmer over very low heat, adding more water as needed, to keep the meat covered. The meat will need to cook for 1½ to 2 hours. Allow to cool in the liquid.

Remove the meat from the liquid and shred it. Toss it with about two-thirds of the lime juice, the cumin seeds, chili powder, oregano, and salt and pepper to taste. Strain the cooking liquid and allow to cool, then lift off the fat which will have solidified on the surface. Reserve this strained cooking liquid for soup.

Brown about half the remaining onion in a tablespoon or two of the olive oil until it is soft. Season with salt and set aside. Sauté the peppers in a small amount of olive oil until they are softened, then set them aside.

Combine the reserved garlic with the reserved onion, and mix it with the tomatoes, cilantro, and green chile. Set aside.

Heat a few tablespoons of the oil in a heavy skillet, then add handfuls of the meat and sauté it over a high heat until crisp and browned, about 5 minutes. This is best done in a nonstick skillet. Repeat until the meat is all crisply browned.

Combine the meat with the fried onions and chopped peppers, and serve with salsa spooned over it and accompanied by wedges of lime, and sour cream and scallions.

Helpful hint

To make Cuban Sandwiches, shred any leftover *Vaca Frita* and put it in a soft roll spread with mayonnaise and mustard. Add a dash of hot sauce, a slice of cheese, some roasted red peppers, a few salad leaves, and some pickled cucumbers. Close up tightly, and brown in a skillet or saucepan with a weight on top, then turn over and brown the other side.

Ingredients

2–2¼ lb (1 kg) flank steak
3 onions, sliced thin
1 carrot, chopped
6 to 8 cloves garlic, chopped
1 to 2 beef bouillon cubes
Salt and pepper to taste
¼–½ cup (60–90 mL) lime juice (or bitter orange juice)
½ tsp cumin seeds
½ tsp mild chili powder, or to taste
½ tsp dried oregano
¼–⅓ cup (45–65 mL) extra-virgin olive oil
1 each: green and red bell pepper, chopped
2 ripe tomatoes, diced (do not use canned)
5 Tbsp (65 mL) fresh chopped cilantro
1 to 2 green chiles, chopped
Wedges of lime and sour cream, to serve
3 scallions, sliced thin

italian meatballs *with peppers*

Serves 4

8 oz (250 g) each: ground beef
  and pork
1 onion, chopped fine
3 to 4 cloves garlic, chopped
6 Tbsp (75 mL) freshly grated
  Parmesan cheese
2 cups (500 mL) bread crumbs
Salt and black pepper
1 Tbsp (15 mL) mixed herbs
Few oregano leaves, crushed
3–4 Tbsp (45–50 mL) fresh
  chopped parsley
1/2 cup (125 mL) tomato juice
4 Tbsp (50 mL) olive oil
1 onion, sliced thin
1 each: green, red, yellow bell
  peppers, sliced thin
1/4 tsp (1 mL) sugar
3–4 Tbsp (45–50 mL) tomato
  paste

Italian meatballs, filled with Parmesan cheese, herbs, onion, and garlic and browned with lots of peppers, make a hearty, comforting meal.

Preparation time: 10–15 minutes Cooking time: 20–25 minutes

In a large bowl combine the ground meat with the chopped onion, half the garlic, the grated cheese, bread crumbs, salt and pepper, half the herbs and oregano, parsley, and 2–4 tablespoons tomato juice. Mix well and form the mixture into meatballs.

Heat a tablespoon or two of the oil in a heavy saucepan or skillet large enough to take all the meatballs, and deep enough to cook the peppers alongside.

Add the meatballs, cooking first on one side, turning carefully to brown all over. When the meatballs are half done (still very red inside) transfer them to a separate dish for a few minutes. Return skillet to the heat and sauté the sliced onion, the remaining garlic, and the peppers, adding more olive oil if needed. Add the sugar to the peppers, some salt and pepper, and the remaining herbs, and cook until the peppers are soft and lightly browned in places. Pour in the remaining tomato juice, cook for a few minutes, then stir in the tomato paste. Return the meatballs to the saucepan, cover, and finish cooking, a further 10 minutes or so.

Taste for seasoning and serve with rice, or crusty bread, to scoop up the sauce.

balkan stuffed *peppers*

Serves 4

12 oz (350 g) ground pork
1 onion, chopped
5 cloves garlic, chopped
2 slices bacon, diced
1/3 cup (50–65 mL) tomato paste
1/3 cup (50–65 mL) cooked rice
1/4–1/2 tsp (1–2 mL) thyme
1/4 tsp (1 mL) ground allspice
Black pepper to taste
Salt if needed
Several pinches cinnamon
4 to 6 small to medium green
  bell peppers, for stuffing
2 cups (500 mL) broth
1 mild red chile, diced fine
2 tsp (10 mL) paprika
5–7 Tbsp (65–80 mL) yogurt

I have approximated the slightly spicy peppers used in Eastern European cooking, by using sweet peppers with the addition of a little fresh chile.

Preparation time: 20 minutes Cooking time: 1–1½ hours

Preheat oven to 375°F (190°C). Mix the ground pork with the onion, garlic, bacon, 2–3 tablespoons tomato paste, rice, thyme, allspice, black pepper, salt if using, and cinnamon. Use this mixture to stuff the peppers and arrange the stuffed peppers in a baking pan, leaving a little space between each pepper.

Pour the broth around the peppers, sprinkle with the chiles, then with paprika, and cover well with foil.

Bake for about an hour or until the peppers are lightly browned on top. Remove from the pan, pour off the sauce from the bottom of the pan into a saucepan, and bring to a boil. Cook over high heat until reduced by about half, then stir in the remaining tomato paste and the yogurt. Taste for seasoning and pour the sauce over the peppers. Serve hot.

bachi's beef, onion, *and green pepper patties*

This marvelous, simple dish of minced beef patties cooked with onions and peppers was one of my grandmother's Sunday night suppers.

Family legend has it that no one in the family knows how she made it; even she claims not to remember. But I watched her every move.

Serves 4

1 lb (500 g) lean ground beef

3 to 4 cloves garlic, coarsely chopped

1 onion, chopped fine

1–2 Tbsp (15–25 mL) vegetable oil, if needed

3 to 4 onions, sliced thin

3 cloves garlic, sliced thin

3 green bell peppers, sliced thin

Soy sauce to taste

Preparation time: 5–10 minutes Cooking time: 20–30 minutes

Mix the meat with the chopped garlic and the chopped onion and form it into small but thick patties.

Heat the oil in a skillet, add the patties, and brown quickly on each side over medium-high heat. Add the onions, sliced garlic, peppers, and soy sauce to taste, then reduce the heat and cook, covered, over low heat for about 20 minutes, turning once halfway through the cooking time.

You should have browned patties, onions, and peppers cooked together with a very small amount of liquid. If the onions and peppers are not browned well enough, remove the meat and sauce and allow the onions and peppers to brown before serving everything together. For extra "bite" you could dust the dish with a sprinkling of paprika.

poultry, meat,
& fish

turkish lamb *and pepper kebobs*

The meat for these kebobs is best marinated for 1 to 2 nights in the refrigerator, but if you are in a rush, 2 hours at room temperature will do.

Preparation time: 10–15 minutes
Marinating time: 2 hours–2 days Cooking time: 5–10 minutes

Combine the meat with the onion, salt and pepper, paprika, Turkish hot pepper paste, tomato paste, mint, thyme, cumin, grated lemon or lime rind, yogurt, lemon juice, and olive oil. Mix well and add the pepper and mild chile quarters to the bowl, mix again, cover and refrigerate for up to 2 days, or leave at room temperature for up to 2 hours.

Combine the relish ingredients in a small bowl and chill.

Thread the meat onto skewers.

Prepare the barbecue or heat the broiler. Cook the meat skewers and marinated peppers to the desired doneness, about 3 to 4 minutes per side. Serve the kebobs with warm pita bread, a spoonful of the relish, the chopped herb mixture, and a spoonful of yogurt.

Serves 4

1 lb (500 g) lean lamb, cut into
  bite-sized pieces
1 onion, minced
Salt and pepper
1 tsp (5 mL) paprika
1 Tbsp (15 mL) Turkish hot
  pepper paste
1 Tbsp (15 mL) tomato paste
1 tsp (5 mL) mint
¼ tsp (1mL) fresh chopped
  thyme
¼ tsp (1 mL) cumin
1 Tbsp (15 mL) grated lemon
  or lime rind
1 Tbsp (15 mL) yogurt
Juice of ½ lemon
2 Tbsp (25 mL) extra-virgin
  olive oil
1 red bell pepper, cut into
  thick wedges
1 to 3 mild chiles, cut
  lengthwise into quarters

RELISH
2 ripe tomatoes, diced
1 green bell pepper, diced
1 onion, chopped fine
¼ chile, chopped fine (optional)

TO SERVE
4–8 pieces pita bread
Handful fresh chopped mint,
  arugula, cilantro, and
  watercress
Yogurt as desired

chiles stuffed *with picadillo*

Chiles rellenos are traditionally filled with cheese, dipped in batter and fried

until crisp, but I like simply to heat them in a baking pan,

and serve them with a spoonful of sour cream, a sprinkling of cilantro,

and some salsa or chopped scallions.

Serves 4

1 onion, chopped

3 cloves garlic, chopped

1 Tbsp (15 mL) olive oil

12 oz (350 g) lean beef

¼–½ tsp (1–2 mL) ground
   cinnamon

½–1 tsp (2–5 mL) mild chili
   powder

Large pinch ground cloves

¼ tsp (1 mL) cumin

Large pinch cayenne to taste

Salt to taste (reduce or omit if
   using salted, roasted almonds)

⅓–½ cup (50–75 mL) each
   seedless raisins and dry-
   roasted almonds

5 Tbsp (65 mL) tomato paste

½ cup (90 mL) dry sherry or dry
   red wine

1–2 Tbsp (15–25 mL) light
   brown sugar, or to taste

Dash vinegar, to taste

2 Tbsp (25 mL) fresh chopped
   cilantro

4 large mild green chiles such
   as poblano or Anaheim,
   roasted

⅓–½ cup (50–75 mL)
   sour cream

Preparation time: 15–20 minutes Cooking time: 20–30 minutes 🌶🌶🌶🌶

Lightly sauté the onion and garlic in the olive oil until softened, then add the meat and lightly brown but do not cook through.

Stir in the cinnamon, chili powder, cloves, cumin, and cayenne. Cook over medium heat for a few minutes, then add the salt, seedless raisins, almonds, tomato paste, sherry or wine, and sugar. Cook over medium heat until the liquid reduces to a thick, saucelike consistency, 15 to 20 minutes then balance the sweetness by adding a little vinegar to taste. Stir in the cilantro.

Preheat the oven to 375°F (190°C).

It depends on the type of pepper you have as to how easy it is to stuff. If the pepper looks as if it may fall apart do not skin it, but you should not eat the skin. It is preferable to peel the chile, leave the stem, but remove the seeds and solid matter inside (do this through a slit on the side — stuff the chiles through this slit).

Arrange the chiles in a baking pan and fill each one with about a quarter of the meat mixture. Any extra meat can be set aside and used as a filling for a taco or sandwich. Cover with foil and bake through, about 20 minutes.

Serve hot with a spoonful of sour cream on top of each stuffed chile. If liked, you can dust with a little paprika.

citrus-spiced fish *with red pepper caponata*

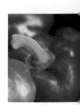

The turmeric-yellow hue of the fish brings out the sunny nature of the lemon, in this Mediterranean-inspired dish; serve with a little caponata, a variation on the traditional Sicilian dish. This spicy version makes a perfect foil for the fish.

Preparation time: 40 minutes
Marinating time: 60 minutes Cooking time: 20–30 minutes

Combine the fish with the garlic, orange juice, lemon juice, cumin, ginger, turmeric, paprika, salt, cayenne pepper, and half the olive oil. Toss to mix well and allow to marinate for 30 to 60 minutes.

In the meantime make the caponata. Lightly sauté the onion, pepper, and sliced garlic in the olive oil until soft. Sprinkle with salt as they cook, then add the tomatoes, jalapeño, cumin, turmeric, ginger, saffron, fennel, and sugar, and continue to cook for about a further 10 minutes, or until thickened and saucelike.

Stir in the capers, olives, seedless raisins, and lemon juice, then taste for seasoning; you want a sweet-sour-spicy balance, so adjust the sugar, lemon juice, and spices accordingly.

Stir in the marjoram or parsley and reserved chopped garlic, taste for seasoning, and allow to cool.

Remove the fish from the marinade, pat dry, and lay on a pan. Brush with the remaining oil and cook under a hot broiler or in a medium-hot grill pan, turning carefully once. Allow only about 5 minutes per side, taking care not to overcook.

Serve the fish with a spoonful of cold red pepper caponata alongside.

Serves 4

FISH

1¾ lb (750 g) cod or haddock fillets

4 cloves garlic, peeled and sliced thin or chopped

Juice of ½ orange or 2 Tbsp orange juice from a carton

Juice of ½ lemon

¼ tsp cumin

⅛ tsp each: ginger, turmeric, paprika

Salt and cayenne pepper to taste

6–7 Tbsp extra-virgin olive oil

CAPONATA

1 onion, sliced thin

1 red bell pepper, chopped

4 cloves garlic: three sliced thin, and one chopped fine

5–6 Tbsp (65–75 mL) extra-virgin olive oil

Salt to taste

4 to 5 ripe tomatoes (canned is fine, use the juice as well)

¼ jalapeño chile, chopped

Pinch each: cumin, turmeric, dried ginger, saffron threads

⅛ tsp (0.5 mL) fennel seeds or ¼ bulb fennel, diced

2 Tbsp sugar (25 mL), or to taste

1–2 Tbsp (15–25 mL) capers in brine, drained, or salted capers, soaked and drained

About 10 green or black Mediterranean olives, pitted and halved

2 Tbsp (25 mL) seedless raisins

Juice of 1 lemon, or to taste

1 Tbsp (15 mL) fresh chopped marjoram and/or parsley

moroccan fish *and pepper brochettes*

Serves 4

5 garlic cloves, chopped

¹/₂ tsp (2 mL) each: paprika and
  cumin

Several pinches cayenne pepper

¹/₂–1 tsp (2–5 mL) salt, or to
  taste

6 Tbsp (75 mL) extra-virgin
  olive oil

2 Tbsp (25 mL) each: fresh
  chopped parsley and cilantro

Juice of 1 lemon

1 lb (500 g) firm-fleshed white
  fish, cut into bite-sized pieces

1 each: red, yellow, green bell
  pepper, peeled, and cut into
  bite-sized pieces

1 lemon, cut into wedges

Charmoula is a Moroccan sauce of sweet roasted peppers, spices, and herbs,

most frequently served with barbecued fish.

Preparation time: 10 minutes
Marinating time: 2 hours–overnight Cooking time: 10 minutes

Combine the garlic, paprika, cumin, cayenne pepper, salt, olive oil, 1 tablespoon of each of the parsley and cilantro, and the lemon juice. Add the fish pieces and mix carefully, until thoroughly coated. Allow to marinate for 2 hours at room temperature or overnight in the refrigerator.

Thread onto skewers alternating with chunks of pepper.

Light the barbecue. Grill the brochettes over charcoal until slightly browned on each side, 7 to 8 minutes in total.

Serve sprinkled with the remaining parsley, cilantro, and lemon wedges. Have hot sauce on the side, for those who enjoy a spicier flavor.

cornmeal-fried trout *with many chiles*

Serves 4

2 mild red chiles, such as
  ancho, mulatto, etc.

4 trout, about 10 oz (300 g)
  each, cleaned

Salt and pepper

¹/₂–1 tsp (2–5 mL) each: mild
  chili powder and paprika

¹/₂ tsp (2 mL) cumin

¹/₄–¹/₃ cup (45–65 mL) cornmeal

2 Tbsp (25 mL) butter

10 cloves garlic, sliced thin

3–4 Tbsp (45–50 mL) extra-
  virgin olive oil

1 each: red bell pepper, mild
  red or orange chile, mild
  green chile, diced

2 cloves garlic, minced

1 lime or lemon, cut into
  wedges

In Mexican cuisine, chiles are occasionally sliced thin

then fried. It gives them a nutty flavor and crisp texture, but

I find that too many can be hard on the digestion.

Preparation time: 15–20 minutes Cooking time: 15–20 minutes

Using scissors, cut the first two chiles in the ingredients list crosswise into very thin strips. Discard the stems and seeds.

Wash the trout and sprinkle outside and inside the cavity with salt, pepper, mild chili powder, paprika, and cumin, then dust them with cornmeal.

Heat the butter in a heavy skillet and brown the trout, adding the thinly sliced chiles to the skillet with the fish. Cook the trout for 6 to 10 minutes, or until the fish just flakes; add the garlic when the fish is half done so that it turns golden rather than browns too darkly. Cook the fish, chiles, and garlic in several batches if necessary. Remove the fish and chiles from the skillet and keep warm.

Rinse the skillet and return to the heat. Add the olive oil and sauté the diced red pepper and the remaining diced chiles for 5 minutes or until tender, then add the minced garlic. Cook for a minute or two, then spoon around the trout. Serve immediately with lime or lemon wedges.

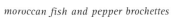

moroccan fish and pepper brochettes

garlic-roasted monkfish *with peppers and saffron cream*

Slices of roast monkfish resting on a bed of red and green peppers in a pool of golden saffron cream – Provence on your plate.

Serves 4

2 heads garlic, broken into cloves and peeled but left whole

1 cup (250 mL) dry white wine

2 lb (1 kg) monkfish, skinned, membrane removed

3 to 4 cloves garlic, sliced thin

Salt and pepper

2 oz (50 g) butter

4 shallots, chopped

3 cloves garlic, chopped

1 each: red and green bell pepper, sliced thin

2 ripe tomatoes, chopped

2–3 tsp (10–15 mL) fresh chopped tarragon

Two pinches saffron threads

2 Tbsp (25 mL) cold water

½ cup (125 mL) fish broth

1 cup (200 mL) sour cream

Preparation time: 20 minutes   Cooking time: 20–30 minutes

Preheat oven to 400°F (200°C).

Combine the whole garlic cloves and wine in a saucepan and bring to a boil. Simmer for about 5 minutes or until the garlic is about half done. Remove and discard the garlic and reserve the wine for making the sauce.

Meanwhile, make little incisions in the fish and insert one or two of the garlic slices into each. Sprinkle with salt and pepper.

Heat half the butter in a heavy skillet and cook the monkfish and garlic cloves for about 1 to 2 minutes per side, turning carefully until lightly browned on all sides. Transfer to a roasting pan and bake for about 15 minutes at 400°F (200°C).

Meanwhile, add the remaining butter to the skillet and lightly sauté the shallots, chopped garlic, and red and green peppers, until softened, 5 to 8 minutes. Stir in the tomatoes and tarragon and cook a few more minutes.

Pour in the reserved garlic-flavored wine and cook over high heat until it is about half evaporated. In a small bowl, soak the saffron in the water; add the broth and continue to cook until it has reduced by about half. Reduce the heat to low, then stir in the sour cream and the soaked saffron and water. Heat through and taste for seasoning. Remove the roasted monkfish from the pan, carve into slices, and serve on a bed of peppers over a pool of sauce.

Helpful hint

Mashed potatoes, with or without garlic, go very well with this dish. Serve with good bread to mop up the sauce, and a green salad.

poultry, meat, & fish

vegetable dishes

Peppers are so widely varied in flavor, texture, and sunny goodness, that they are a great friend of the vegetable table. A panful of peppers alongside onions, zucchini, eggplant, and tomatoes make a summery lunch with lots of leftovers to perk up days of eating.

catalan-style *roasted vegetables*

Serves 4

1 eggplant, cut into 3 or 4 chunks
1 to 2 small to medium-sized red
  onions, peeled and quartered
2 red bell peppers, quartered
1 each: yellow and green bell
  pepper, quartered
3 to 4 zucchini, cut into 2 or
  3 pieces each
2 heads garlic, cloves separated
  but not peeled
4 small ripe tomatoes, cut
  crosswise into half
4–5 Tbsp (50–65 mL) extra-
  virgin olive oil
Small pinch sugar
Salt to taste
Pinch black pepper
4 to 6 cloves garlic, chopped
Handful fresh basil, sliced thin
  or torn
Balsamic vinegar to taste

This is such an easy dish, and so refreshing. Bake in an earthenware dish and double or even triple the recipe. Leftovers are delicious in sandwiches, on ciabatta or focaccia, or added to soups, pasta, salsas, or stews.

Preparation time: 10–15 minutes Cooking time: 45–60 minutes

Preheat oven to 375°F (180°C).

Toss the eggplant, onion quarters, peppers, zucchini, whole garlic cloves, tomatoes, and about 1½ tablespoons of olive oil, sugar, and salt and pepper to taste. Arrange in a baking pan and bake for 45 to 60 minutes, turning occasionally, until the vegetables are evenly roasted.

About 10 minutes before they are ready, sprinkle with the chopped garlic, basil, and balsamic vinegar. Return to the oven to heat through.

Serve warm, at room temperature, or cold as a sandwich filling.

sicilian-style potatoes *and peppers*

Serves 4

4 small to medium-sized
  potatoes, peeled and cut
  into wedges
⅓–½ cup (50 mL) extra-virgin
  olive oil
1 each: red, yellow, green bell
  peppers, sliced
2 onions, sliced thin
Salt and pepper
3 to 5 cloves garlic, chopped
8 to 10 ripe tomatoes, diced
Pinch sugar
2 Tbsp (25 mL) capers,
  preferably salted, soaked in
  cold water for 5 minutes
  then drained

This colorful dish can also be served as an appetizer or a flavorful accompaniment.

Preparation time: 20 minutes Cooking time: 25–30 minutes

Brown the potatoes in the olive oil over medium-high heat until just golden, then add the peppers, onions, and salt and pepper, cover, and continue to cook over medium-low heat until the peppers are soft.

Add half the garlic, the tomatoes, and the sugar and increase the heat to medium or medium-high. Cook, uncovered, until the tomatoes have reduced to a thick saucelike mixture. Add the remaining garlic and the capers and cook for a minute or two longer. Taste for seasoning and serve hot, warm, or at room temperature.

gratin of peppers *and eggplant*

This simple dish of red and yellow peppers and eggplant, bound together with crispy bread crumbs and grated cheese, is from the South of Italy.

Preparation time: 30 minutes Cooking time: 30 minutes

Preheat the oven to 400°F (200°C).

Sprinkle the salt onto the eggplant. Combine the eggplant, olive oil, onion, peppers, tomatoes, about three-quarters of the garlic, the oregano or marjoram, parsley, bread crumbs, and cheese and toss well. Arrange in a roasting pan and bake for about an hour, turning every so often, until the vegetables brown and fall apart a little, forming a thick mixture. If the vegetables seem too dry, add a little more diced tomato and olive oil.

Serve either hot or at room temperature, sprinkled with the remaining garlic, oregano or marjoram, and parsley.

Serves 4

Salt

1 eggplant, cut into bite-sized chunks

6 Tbsp (75 mL) extra-virgin olive oil, or as desired

1 onion, sliced thin

2 red bell peppers, cut into bite-sized pieces

1 yellow bell pepper, cut into bite-sized pieces

4 to 6 ripe tomatoes, diced or 10-oz (284-mL) can chopped tomatoes, including the juices

8 cloves garlic, chopped finely

1–2 tsp (5–10 mL) fresh chopped oregano or marjoram, plus extra for sprinkling

1–2 Tbsp (15–25 mL) fresh chopped parsley, plus extra for sprinkling

5–6 Tbsp (65–75 mL) each: bread crumbs and grated Parmesan or pecorino cheese

black bean *and many-pepper chili*

Serves 6

14 oz (400 g) black beans
6¼ cups (1.5 L) water
2½ cups (600 mL) broth
2 dried mild red chiles, sliced
2 Tbsp (25 mL) olive oil
2 red bell peppers, diced
½ green and yellow bell pepper,
  diced
1 onion, chopped
½ carrot, diced
8 cloves garlic, chopped
2 tsp (10 mL) mild chili powder
1 Tbsp (15 mL) cumin
1 tsp (5 mL) oregano
1 Tbsp (15 mL) paprika
14 oz (400 g) tomatoes, chopped
1 red or green chile, such as
  Anaheim, chopped
⅓–½ cup (50–75 mL) fresh
  chopped cilantro

This black bean chili, rich with sweet and spicy peppers, is delicious on its own in a bowl topped with sour cream, crisp tortilla chips, chopped onions, and grated cheese. It is also good as a sauce for most barbecued dishes and, thinned with broth, it makes a hearty soup.

Preparation time: 15 minutes Cooking time: 2 hours

Put the beans and water in a saucepan and bring to a boil. Reduce the heat and cook until the beans are nearly tender, then add the broth and dried chiles, and continue to cook, adding more liquid if needed.

Pour the olive oil into a skillet and sauté the peppers, onion, carrot, and half the garlic, until softened. Sprinkle with chili powder, cumin, oregano, and paprika, and add the tomatoes. Cook for a few moments, then add to the simmering and almost-tender beans along with the remaining garlic and half the cilantro.

Continue to cook until the beans are very tender and the sauce is rich and dark. Add the fresh chile to taste. Serve sprinkled with the remaining cilantro.

red peppers stuffed *with curried mashed vegetables*

Serves 4

4 red bell peppers, or large mild
  red chiles
5 cloves garlic, chopped
Salt
3 large potatoes, peeled and
  chopped
Spear of broccoli, diced
½ carrot, diced
6 Tbsp (75 mL) butter
½ to 1 fresh chile, chopped
½ tsp (2 mL) curry powder
¼ tsp (1 mL) each: turmeric
  and cumin
6 Tbsp (75 mL) yogurt
2 Tbsp (25 mL) chopped
  cilantro

Curry spices and hot peppers balance with cool, refreshing yogurt and mashed potatoes for this unusual dish of stuffed peppers.

Preparation time: 20–25 minutes Cooking time: 30 minutes

Roast the peppers whole, then peel and remove their seeds through a slit on one side of the pepper, leaving the stems intact if possible. Sprinkle with about a third of the garlic and salt, and set aside.

Cook the potatoes in boiling salted water until just tender, then drain. Cook the broccoli for about 5 minutes in boiling water until tender and brightly colored but still crisp, drain, then cook the carrot until tender and bright in color; drain.

Mash the potatoes and mix them with the butter, broccoli, and carrot, the remaining garlic, chile, spices, half the yogurt, half the cilantro, and salt to taste. Add more yogurt, if necessary, to achieve a spoonable consistency.

Preheat oven to 375°F (190°C). Stuff each pepper gently so as not to tear the flesh. Arrange them in a shallow baking pan, cover tightly with foil, and bake for about 15 minutes.

Serve hot, sprinkled with the remaining cilantro.

black bean and many-pepper chili

93

mixed pepper stir-fry with tofu
and walnuts in sweet and sour sauce

Crisp squares of golden fried tofu and roasted

walnuts with multicolored peppers served with traditional

sweet and sour sauce and a bowl of rice.

Serves 4

12 oz (350 g) tofu, cut into
bite-sized pieces

⅓ cup (50–65 mL) vegetable oil
for frying the tofu in the wok,
more if you're using a
flat skillet

¼ cup (45–50 mL) walnut
pieces

3–4 Tbsp (45–50 mL) dark
brown sugar

2 Tbsp (25 mL) granulated
sugar

6 Tbsp (75 mL) hard cider
vinegar or white wine vinegar

½ cup (125 mL) pineapple juice

2 Tbsp (25 mL) ketchup

1 tsp (5 mL) chopped ginger
root

1 Tbsp (65 mL) cornstarch
mixed with 5 Tbsp (65 mL)
cold water

2 Tbsp (25 mL) oil for stir-
frying or as needed

1 carrot, sliced diagonally

1 onion, cut lengthwise into
wedges or slices

1½ each: green, red, yellow or
orange bell peppers, cut into
bite-sized pieces

3 to 4 tomatoes, cut into
wedges

Soy sauce to taste

Preparation time: 20–25 minutes Cooking time: 15–20 minutes

Dry the tofu pieces thoroughly on paper towels. Heat the oil in a wok and when very hot fry the tofu pieces over medium heat until golden brown on one side, then turn them and cook the other side until golden. Remove from the wok and place on paper towels to drain.

Deep-fry the walnuts in the wok for only a minute or so until golden brown (take care they do not burn, which they are apt to do quite easily). Remove with a slotted spoon and place on paper towels to drain. Remove the wok from the heat.

Make the sweet and sour sauce: combine the dark brown sugar in a saucepan with the granulated sugar, vinegar, pineapple juice, ketchup, and ginger. Bring to a boil and cook for about 5 minutes or until slightly syrupy. Remove from the heat and stir in the cornstarch mixed with water. Set aside.

Return the wok to the heat, you should have about 1 inch (2.5 cm) oil covering the bottom of the wok, remove or replenish oil as needed. Stir-fry the carrots for a minute or two then add the onions and stir-fry until both vegetables are lightly browned in spots, then add the peppers and tomatoes and stir-fry until all the vegetables are crisp and tender, just a moment or two.

Add the tofu and the sweet and sour sauce, and cook for about 5 minutes until the tofu has heated through and the sauce has thickened. Season with soy sauce to taste, sprinkle with the walnuts, and serve.

mixed pepper stir-fry with tofu
and walnuts in sweet and sour sauce

huevos *rancheros*

Mexico's favorite egg dish can be made in a variety of ways but usually includes chiles, and often tomatoes. Serve with pinto or black beans, rice, a little fresh salsa, and a stack of warm tortillas on the side.

Serves 4

1 onion, chopped

3 to 5 cloves garlic, chopped

3–4 Tbsp (45–50 mL) vegetable oil

1 to 2 green bell peppers, sliced thin

3 mild green chiles such as Anaheim or poblano, roasted and sliced

1 to 2 fresh green chiles, such as Kenya or jalapeño, chopped (optional)

2 lb (1 kg) ripe tomatoes, diced or 14-oz (398-mL) can chopped tomatoes

Few fresh oregano leaves, crushed

$^1/_4$–$^1/_2$ tsp (1–2 mL) cumin

Salt to taste

Pinch of sugar

$^1/_2$–1 tsp (2–5 mL) mild chili powder, or to taste

4 or 8 eggs (1 or 2 eggs per person)

4 or 8 tortillas (1 or 2 per person)

3–4 Tbsp (45–50 mL) fresh chopped cilantro

Preparation time: 20 minutes Cooking time: 20 minutes

Lightly sauté the onion and garlic in the oil until softened, then add the peppers, chiles, and tomatoes and cook for a few minutes until the mixture is saucelike.

Purée half the mixture with the oregano, cumin, salt, sugar, and chili powder, then return it to the pot with the reserved sautéed vegetables.

Cook over medium heat until the sauce has reduced, stirring so that it does not stick or burn. Remove from the heat, season, and keep warm.

Meanwhile, poach or fry the eggs and warm the tortillas either in a microwave or heavy lightly oiled skillet.

Serve the eggs on top of the warmed tortillas, with the warm sauce spooned over. Sprinkle with cilantro and serve immediately.

vegetable dishes

red pepper *and tomato soufflé*

This is a wonderful soufflé to make when you have a batch of already made *Coulis de Poivrons Rouges aux Tomates* on hand, although it is worth making the coulis from scratch, just for this recipe.

Preparation time: 15–20 minutes Cooking time: 15–20 minutes

Preheat the oven to 425°F (220°C). Butter the molds generously and coat well with the grated cheese. Set aside.

Whisk the egg whites with the salt until they form stiff, glossy peaks. Whisk the yolks with half the coulis.

Stir a large spoonful of the whites into the egg yolk and coulis mixture, to lighten it, then fold the mixture into the whites. Gently pour or spoon this into the prepared molds.

Bake for 15 to 20 minutes or until the soufflés are puffed up and slightly golden. A soufflé rises because the air trapped inside the little pockets of whipped egg whites expands. Take care if opening the oven door to see if the soufflés are done – if the oven temperature falls, your soufflés could collapse, so open the door gently and briefly.

Serve the hot soufflés immediately, with the remaining coulis on the side.

Serves 4

Butter for the individual soufflé molds
5–6 Tbsp (65–75 mL) grated Parmesan or similar grating cheese
6 eggs, at room temperature, separated
Large pinch salt
1 batch Coulis de Poivrons Rouges aux Tomatoes (p. 131)

vegetable

green beans *with red peppers and balsamic vinegar*

Strands of sweet red pepper add their distinctive flavor to crisp tender green beans. This is a delicious side dish, quick to assemble, and also very attractive.

Serves 4

Salt

Pinch sugar

12 oz (350 g) green beans, trimmed

1 Tbsp (15 mL) extra-virgin olive oil, or as desired

½ onion, chopped

½ red bell pepper, sliced thin or chopped

2 cloves garlic, chopped

Black pepper to taste

¼–½ tsp (1–2 mL) balsamic vinegar

Preparation time: 5–10 minutes Cooking time: 10–15 minutes

Bring a saucepan of water to a boil, add a pinch of salt and sugar, and blanch the green beans briefly until bright green and crisp. Drain and rinse well in cold water. Drain again and set aside.

In the olive oil lightly sauté the onion, then add the pepper and garlic and cook briefly. Add the drained green beans and salt and pepper to taste. Stir and cook for a few minutes then add the balsamic vinegar and remove from the heat. Cover for a minute or two, then serve warm or at room temperature.

basque hot pepper *cauliflower*

This dish is from the Basque village of Esplette. It is traditionally made with the chile which is native to the area. During the October chile festival you might find this on the menu. If the combination of the chile and garlic will be too hot, cut down the quantities.

Preparation time: 10–15 minutes Cooking time: 20 minutes

Chop the pepper, chile, and garlic into a finely diced mixture, then sauté half of this in the olive oil with salt to taste, in a heavy skillet over medium-low heat.

Add the cauliflower and stir-fry until it is tender but still crisp, then add the thyme, tomato paste, and water and cook, covered, for about 10 minutes or long enough for the cauliflower to be completely tender.

Add the rest of the chopped pepper–garlic mixture and cook to warm through; squeeze on the lemon juice and serve warm or at room temperature

Serves 4

1 red bell pepper, roasted, peeled, and chopped

½ to 1 mild red chile (such as poblano), chopped

4 to 5 cloves garlic, chopped

5 Tbsp (65 mL) extra-virgin olive oil

Salt to taste

1 cauliflower, cut into florets

¼ tsp (1 mL) fresh chopped thyme, or to taste

2 Tbsp (25 mL) tomato paste

½ cup (90 mL) water, or as needed

Juice of ¼ to ½ lemon

mexican mashed potatoes *with green peppers and chiles*

The olive oil enhances the potatoes and lets the strong spicy flavors of the peppers, chile, and garlic shine through. Serve with any simple barbecued meat or fish, or with lemon chicken.

Preparation time: 10–15 minutes Cooking time: 30–45 minutes

Roast the green peppers over an open flame until evenly charred, then place them in a tightly sealed plastic bag or a bowl for about 30 minutes. When cool enough to handle, remove the skin, stems, and seeds, but retain any smoky flavored juices that accumulate. Shred the flesh and combine with the green chile, garlic, olive oil, lemon juice, cumin seeds, and salt and cayenne or black pepper. Set aside.

Cook the potatoes in boiling salted water until just tender. Drain. When cool enough to handle, mash coarsely and combine with the roasted peppers and their juices, then toss in the parsley and cilantro. Season to taste and serve at cool room temperature.

Serves 6

2 green bell peppers

½ to 1 green chile, chopped or sliced thin

5 cloves garlic, chopped

⅓–½ cup (65–75 mL) extra-virgin olive oil, or more as desired

Lemon juice to taste

Large pinch cumin seeds

Salt and cayenne or black pepper to taste

3½ lb (1.5 kg) potatoes, preferably waxy ones, cleaned but unpeeled, cut into halves or quarters

¼ cup (45 mL) each: fresh chopped parsley and cilantro

chile-spiced *broccoli*

Serves 4

1 large or 2 medium-sized
  bunches broccoli, broken into
  florets, the stems peeled and
  cut into bite-sized pieces
Pinch sugar
Salt to taste
2 Tbsp (25 mL) extra-virgin
  olive oil
3 to 5 cloves garlic, sliced thin
1 medium-hot or mild fresh red
  chile, or more as desired,
  sliced thin or chopped
Juice of ¼ to ½ lemon
  or to taste
Grated Parmesan cheese
  (optional)

This dish is from southern Italy. Use a chile that is not too hot, with just enough bite to make it "*all'arrabbiata*" (angry), the term given in Italy to chile-spiced dishes. The spicy broccoli can be mixed into spaghetti.

Preparation time: 10 minutes Cooking time: 10–15 minutes

Blanch the broccoli in boiling water to which a pinch of both sugar and salt have been added. Cook for only a minute or two, or until the broccoli is crisp-tender and bright green. Remove from the heat, rinse well in cold water, and dry.

In a wok or large skillet heat the olive oil, garlic, and chile, and warm through, then add the broccoli and cook together, seasoning with a little salt, for a few minutes to meld the flavors. Squeeze the lemon juice over the vegetables and remove from the heat.

Serve the broccoli and red chiles hot, with a grating of Parmesan cheese if wished, or at room temperature, with a little more lemon juice drizzled over the top.

ethiopian *vegetable stew*

Serves 4

3 to 5 shallots, chopped
1–3 tsp (5–15 mL) butter
2 Tbsp (50 mL) tomato paste
1 green bell pepper, sliced thin
½ to 1 carrot, cut into bite-sized
  pieces
2 potatoes, peeled and cut into
  bite-sized pieces
¼ cabbage, cut into small
  bite-sized pieces
6 cardamom pods or 3 pinches
  powdered cardamom
¼ tsp (1 mL) turmeric
½ cup (125 mL) water
3 cloves garlic, chopped
1 tsp (5 mL) chopped ginger root
½ tsp (2 mL) mild red chili
  powder
¼–½ tsp (1–2 mL) hot pepper
  flakes
½ red bell pepper, diced
Salt and black pepper to taste

Peppers sweet, spicy, and hot, feature prominently in many Ethiopian dishes — sauces, salads, soups, stews, and especially raw meat or fish pastes. This is a mild mixed-vegetable stew which is good with rice. In Ethiopia it would be served with *injera*, a flat pancakelike bread.

Preparation time: 15–20 minutes Cooking time: 15–20 minutes

Sauté the shallots in the butter, covered, until softened and light golden brown then stir in the tomato paste, green pepper, carrot, potato, cabbage, cardamom, turmeric, and water. Stir, cover, and cook for 10 minutes.

Mince the garlic and ginger then add half to the simmering vegetables with the chili powder, the hot pepper flakes, and the red pepper. Cover again and return to a simmer, adding more water if needed. Season to taste with salt and black pepper.

Cook for a further 10 to 15 minutes or until the vegetables are quite tender. Remove from the heat, stir in the remaining garlic-ginger paste, and serve.

roasted sweet *potatoes with red pepper-lime butter*

Tender roasted sweet potatoes with melting

chile-butter is a perfect dish to serve in the fall.

Serves 4

4 sweet potatoes, preferably
  orange-fleshed
1 red pepper, roasted, peeled,
  and diced
3 to 4 cloves garlic, chopped
1–2 Tbsp (15–25 mL) olive oil
1 tsp mild chili powder
¼ tsp (1 mL) cumin, or more
  to taste
8 Tbsp (90 mL) butter, at room
  temperature or softened
Salt to taste
Juice of ½ lime, or to taste

Preparation time: 5 minutes
Cooking time: 40 minutes conventional oven,
15 minutes if using microwave and conventional oven

Preheat the oven to 375°F (190°C).

Roast the sweet potatoes in the oven, in their skins, for about 40 minutes or until they are just tender. Alternatively, microwave them for about 5 minutes on high, then transfer them to the oven and roast at 400°F (200°C) for about 10 minutes.

Meanwhile, make the red pepper-lime butter. Mix the pepper with the garlic, olive oil, chili powder, and cumin until it forms a thick mixture, then work in the soft butter. Taste for seasoning, then add salt and lime juice as desired.

Serve this pepper butter spooned into each potato, or serve the sweet potatoes cut into thick slices with a piece of the butter on top.

fried rice with peppers, *water chestnuts, and peas*

Fried rice is a classic of the Chinese kitchen, in all areas where they eat rice.

Leftovers from the daily rice pot are often fried and served like this.

Preparation time: 15–20 minutes Cooking time: 15–20 minutes

Cook the rice in the water until it is just tender and the water has been absorbed. Do this at least an hour ahead of time, preferably a day ahead of time and store it in the refrigerator. Leftover rice definitely makes the best fried rice; freshly cooked rice tends to turn mushy.

Stir-fry the garlic and ginger in a wok or skillet in about a tablespoon of the oil then add the peppers, celery, and water chestnuts. Sprinkle with sugar and salt, and stir-fry until they are crisply cooked, only a few minutes. Add the peas or green pepper, stir for a few moments, then remove from the wok.

Add another tablespoon of oil, heat, then add the rice to the wok in one layer, and let the bottom brown then turn it once or twice so that you have large pieces of browned rice chunks. Push the rice to one side of the wok, add the remaining oil, then pour in the eggs and a drizzle of soy sauce. Cook the eggs, scrambling them on the bottom of the wok away from the rice, letting a little of the eggs blend with the rice but most of the eggs form small, delicious curds.

When the eggs are done, toss them into the rice, return the vegetables to the wok, and season everything with soy sauce and sesame oil to taste. Turn out onto a plate and sprinkle generously with scallions and cilantro. Serve immediately.

Serves 4

1 cup (250 mL) long-grain
   white rice
1 cup (250 mL) water,
   or as needed
3 to 4 cloves garlic, chopped
1–2 tsp (5–10 mL) finely
   chopped ginger root
2 Tbsp (25 mL) vegetable oil, or
   as needed
1 to 2 red bell peppers, diced
1 stalk celery, diced
3½ oz (100 g) water chestnuts,
   cut into quarters or cubes
Pinch sugar and salt
⅔ cup (130 mL) peas (frozen is
   fine) or 1 green bell pepper,
   diced
2 eggs, lightly beaten
Soy sauce to taste
Generous drizzle sesame oil
3 scallions, sliced thin
2 Tbsp (25 mL) fresh chopped
   cilantro

alexa's pepper-studded *risotto alla milanese*

Serves 4

2 shallots, chopped

2 cloves garlic, chopped

4 Tbsp (50 mL) butter

1½ to 2 each: yellow, red, green, orange bell peppers, diced

1 cup (250 mL) arborio rice

2½ cups (600 mL) hot chicken broth

1¼ cups (300 mL) dry white wine

2 pinches saffron threads, dissolved in 2 Tbsp (25 mL) water

6 Tbsp (75 mL) freshly grated Parmesan cheese, or as desired

1 Tbsp (15 mL) fresh chopped flat leaf parsley

Salt and pepper

This risotto — concocted by cookbook editor and friend Alexa Stace — is yellow as a tropical sunset, scented with saffron, and studded with peppers.

Preparation time: 15 minutes   Cooking time: 45 minutes

Lightly sauté the shallots and garlic in the butter until softened, then add half of the peppers and cook for a minute or two, stirring.

Using a wooden spoon, stir in the rice, cook briefly, then pour ⅔ cup (50 ml) of the hot broth into the rice, stirring constantly as it cooks. When the liquid has been absorbed, add more broth, and continue stirring and cooking until this too has been absorbed. Continue this gradual adding of liquid and stirring, moving on to the wine in about 3 batches, after you have used up all the broth.

After the first addition of wine, stir in the reserved peppers, and the saffron with its yellow-colored water and add another slosh of wine. Keep stirring and cooking, and add the remaining wine. When the risotto is ready, your grains of rice will be bound by a creamy sauce. It should not be too thick, however, so add more water, broth, or wine if it looks too glutinous.

A risotto takes about 30 minutes to cook; some rices take less, say 25, while others take substantially more, perhaps 45–50 minutes.

When the rice grains are al dente (tender but still firm to the bite) stir in the cheese and parsley. Season to taste with salt and pepper and serve immediately.

cypriot bulghur *wheat pilaf*

Serves 4

1 onion, chopped

5 cloves garlic, chopped

1 green bell pepper, diced

½ to 1 mild red chile, chopped

½ to 1 yellow bell pepper, diced

2 Tbsp (25 mL) olive oil

1¼ cups (250 mL) bulghur wheat

8 ripe tomatoes, diced,

1¼ cups (300 mL) chicken or vegetable broth

Several pinches oregano

Pinch of cumin (optional)

Salt and black pepper

1 Tbsp (15 mL) fresh chopped parsley

Serve with a salad of chopped mixed greens, diced green peppers, cucumbers, and black olives, with a bowl of yogurt on the side.

Preparation time: 15–20 minutes   Cooking time: 20–25 minutes

Sauté the onion, garlic, peppers, and chile in the olive oil until lightly browned, then add the bulghur, stir to coat well, and lightly toast over the heat.

Add the tomatoes, broth, oregano, and cumin if using, bring to a boil, then cover and cook for a few minutes. Remove from the heat to absorb the flavors. The bulghur will either be ready to eat now, or need a few minutes more cooking time. Season with salt and pepper, and fork through to fluff up. Serve sprinkled with parsley.

red pepper, corn, *and cheese polenta*

Instant polenta may not be as flavorful as the original long-cooking variety,

but is very convenient, and just as sumptuous.

Preparation time: 15–20 minutes
Cooking time: 15–20 minutes instant polenta;
40–45 minutes conventional long-cooking polenta

Serves 4

Lightly sauté the peppers, onion, and garlic in the olive oil until softened, then stir in the polenta grains and cook them lightly in the olive oil, allowing them to absorb the flavor of the oil, and cook slightly.

Stir in the water, about a third at a time, letting it cook and absorb between additions, and when about half the water has been absorbed stir in the salt, rosemary, corn, and tomatoes, then continue with the water until it reaches a soft, thick consistency. This will take 5 to 8 minutes if using instant polenta, and about 30 minutes if using the long-cooking variety.

Stir in the cheeses and hot sauce to taste, and serve in bowls, with extra cheese on the side if wished.

Helpful hint

Turn this into a California classic, tamale pie, by adding broken up browned lean ground beef and mild chili spices such as ancho or New Mexico chili powder, or a mixture of mild chili powder and paprika. Pour it into a pan, top it with grated cheese, and bake until it melts and sizzles.

2 red bell peppers, diced
1 onion, chopped
5 cloves garlic, chopped
¼ cup (45 mL) extra-virgin olive oil
1½ cups (375 mL) instant or ordinary long-cooking polenta
1 quart (1 L) boiling water
Salt to taste
3 to 5 small sprigs fresh rosemary, stems removed, the leaves chopped (2 to 3 tsp)
1 cup (250 mL) cooked corn kernels (frozen or canned is fine)
14-oz (398-mL) can chopped tomatoes, including the juices, or about 8 ripe flavorful fresh tomatoes, diced
3 cups (750 mL) grated Jarlsburg or Gruyère cheese
6 Tbsp (75 mL) grated Parmesan cheese, or to taste
Hot sauce or black pepper, to taste

potato-goat cheese gratin *with chipotle cream*

Serves 4

3 lb (1½ kg) baking potatoes, peeled and cut into chunks
Salt and pepper
Scant 1 cup (200 mL) sour cream
½ cup (125 mL) vegetable broth
4 cloves garlic, chopped
1–2 tsp (5–10 mL) marinade from chipotles en adobo, or ½ chopped chipotle or mild chili powder to taste
8 oz (200 g) goat cheese, sliced
1½ cups (375 mL) melting white cheese such as Queso Anejo, medium Asiago, Monterey Jack or Mozzarella, shredded
½–¾ cup (125–175 mL) Parmesan or pecorino, shredded

This makes a luscious casserole of potatoes baked with tangy goat's cheese and piquant chipotle, rich with cream and melted cheese. Serve with a crisp salad lightly dressed with olive oil and vinegar.

Preparation time: 20 minutes Cooking time: 45 minutes

Preheat oven to 350–375°F (170–180°C).

Cook the potatoes in rapidly boiling water until half done. Drain and sprinkle with salt and pepper.

Combine the sour cream with the broth, half the garlic, and the chipotle marinade, chipotle or chili powder.

Arrange half the potatoes in a baking casserole then pour half the sour cream sauce over the potatoes. Add a layer of goat cheese, then finish with the remaining potatoes and sauce.

Sprinkle with shredded white cheese then with shredded Parmesan or pecorino.

Bake in oven until the potatoes are creamy inside and the cheese topping is lightly golden and crisped in places on top. Serve immediately, sprinkled with the remaining garlic.

balkan eggs with *peppers, feta cheese, and tomatoes*

Serves 4

12 oz (350 g) feta cheese, cut into thick slices
4 to 6 ripe tomatoes, cut into slices or wedges
½ each: red and green bell peppers, sliced very thin or chopped
3 cloves garlic, chopped
1½–2 Tbsp (20–25 mL) extra-virgin olive oil or butter
2 to 4 pickled mild or medium-hot peppers, such as jalapeños en escabeche or Turkish pickled peppers, sliced
4 or 8 eggs (1 or 2 per person)
Pinch paprika
Pinch thyme

This Bulgarian dish makes an excellent appetizer or supper dish, especially if served in little individual ceramic casseroles. Diners can lift off the lid and inhale the enticing aroma as the steam wafts up from the casserole dish.

Preparation time: 15 minutes Cooking time: 20 minutes

Preheat the oven to 400°F (200°C).

Arrange the cheese, tomatoes, and peppers in the bottom of 4 individual or 1 shallow baking dish. Sprinkle with garlic, half the olive oil or butter, and pickled peppers. Bake for 5 to 8 minutes or long enough to heat through and lightly cook the vegetables.

Remove from the heat and break 1 or 2 eggs into each serving of vegetables and cheese. Spoon a little of the cheese vegetable mixture over each egg, sprinkle with paprika and thyme, and the remaining oil or butter, and cover with either a lid or foil.

Bake until the eggs are set, about 8 minutes. Serve immediately, steaming hot, with plenty of country bread.

pasta

Pasta goes beautifully with peppers. With pasta and peppers in your cupboard, you need very little else to make a satisfying meal. Always cook pasta until al dente (tender, but still firm to the bite).

ravioli and peppers *with spicy tomato sauce*

Ham-filled ravioli work best in this dish, but if you wish to use a

pasta with a different filling, choose any that has a good, strong flavor.

Spinach ravioli would be excellent, or pumpkin.

Serves 4

2 green bell peppers, cut into
  quarters
5 Tbsp (65 mL) extra-virgin
  olive oil
2 onions, sliced thin lengthwise
Pinch salt to taste
14-oz (398-mL) can tomatoes
  or 1¼ lb (600 g) fresh
  tomatoes, diced
Pinch sugar to taste
4 cloves garlic, minced
½ tsp (2 mL) cumin, or to taste
Hot pepper flakes to taste,
  or 1 small hot red or green
  chile, chopped
1 each: red and yellow bell
  pepper, diced
About 1 lb (500 g) fresh
  ham-filled ravioli

Preparation time: 15 minutes Cooking time: 20 minutes

Lightly char the green peppers skin-side down in the hot oil, then turn them over and add the onions and a sprinkling of salt. Continue to cook over medium high heat until the onions are lightly browned in places. Add the tomatoes and a pinch of sugar, reduce the heat, and cook until the mixture is thick and saucelike.

Remove from the heat and add the garlic, cumin, and hot pepper flakes or fresh hot chile. Set aside.

Add the red and yellow peppers to a large pot of rapidly boiling salted water, then add the ravioli and cook until they are just cooked through, about 5 minutes depending on the ravioli.

Drain the ravioli and diced peppers and toss with the pepper and tomato sauce. Serve immediately.

fettucine with pumpkin *and red pepper sauce*

This elegant sauce is rich with pumpkin, sweet red peppers, and cream, and can be prepared up to two days in advance. Reheat it and thin it with a little water when you cook the pasta.

Preparation time: 15–20 minutes Cooking time: 20 minutes

Lightly sauté the onion or shallots and garlic in the butter until just softened, then add the pumpkin and sauté until it is lightly browned and almost tender. Add the red pepper and continue to cook for a few minutes until both vegetables are soft.

Add the broth, increase the heat to high, and cook until the liquid has reduced by about three-quarters, then stir in the cream and add the thyme and black and cayenne pepper. Lower the heat to a simmer while you cook the pasta.

Cook the pasta in rapidly boiling salted water until al dente (tender, but still firm to the bite), then drain. Toss the pasta with the sauce, top each portion with grated Parmesan cheese and a sprinkling of ground black pepper, and serve immediately.

Serves 4

1 onion or 3 to 5 shallots, chopped
1 clove garlic, chopped
4 Tbsp (50 mL) butter
14 oz (400 g) pumpkin or winter squash, peeled and diced
1½ red bell peppers, diced
1 cup (250 mL) vegetable or chicken broth
1¼–1½ cups (300–350 mL) heavy cream
Pinch thyme
Pinch each: black and cayenne pepper to taste
12–14 oz (350–400 g) dried fettucine or 1 lb (500 g) fresh fettucine
Salt as needed
Freshly grated Parmesan cheese to serve

bayou gnocchi

Serves 4

1 each: green and yellow bell
  pepper, diced
$1/2$ to 1 mild red chile, chopped
5 Tbsp (65 mL) extra-virgin
  olive oil
2 kielbasa or other smoked
  sausages, approximately 8 oz
  (200 g)
3 to 5 cloves garlic, chopped
14-oz (398-mL) can tomatoes
2 Tbsp (25 mL) tomato paste
$1/4$ tsp (1 mL) mixed herbs
14-oz (398-mL) can red kidney
  beans, drained and rinsed
$1/4$ tsp (1 mL) oregano
Black pepper to taste
Salt if needed
1 lb (500 g) gnocchi
3–4 Tbsp (45–50 mL) fresh
  chopped parsley
Parmesan cheese to taste

Chunky gnocchi in a sauce smoky with sausage, rich with green and yellow peppers, and tangy with tomatoes and plenty of garlic. It is a hearty dish, easy to prepare, and blends the flavors of Louisiana with those of Italy.

Preparation time: 10–15 minutes Cooking time: 20 minutes

Sauté the peppers and the chile in the olive oil until lightly browned. Slice the sausage into $1/2$–$3/4$-in (1–2-cm) pieces and add to the pan with the garlic, cook for a few minutes then add the tomatoes, tomato paste, herbs, and kidney beans. Simmer over medium-low heat, until the mixture is flavorful and thick, about 15 minutes. Season to taste with black pepper and, sparingly, with salt if needed.

Cook the gnocchi in salted water until they bob to the surface (1 to 2 minutes) then drain and toss with the sauce, parsley, and cheese. Serve immediately.

pasta with hot pepper sauce *and black olives*

Serves 4

$2/3$–$3/4$ cup (150–175 mL) extra-
  virgin olive oil
3 to 6 mild red chiles, chopped
14-oz (398-mL) can tomatoes,
  chopped
Salt and pepper to taste
Pinch sugar
10 cloves garlic, chopped or
  minced with a sprinkling or
  two of salt
12 oz (350 g) spaghetti
Freshly grated Parmesan or
  pecorino cheese, to taste
3–4 Tbsp (45–50 mL) tapénade

Choose the number of chiles according to how hot they are and how spicy you want the sauce to be.

Preparation time: 10–15 minutes Cooking time: 50–55 minutes

Place the olive oil and chiles in a saucepan and heat gently, allowing the peppers to cook but not fry. Cook over medium-low heat for 10 to 15 minutes; they will turn color and lightly stew. Add the tomatoes, salt, pepper, sugar, and about half the garlic. Continue to simmer for about 30 minutes or until the mixture is a thickened, saucelike purée. Add the remaining garlic.

Cook the pasta in boiling salted water until al dente (tender, but still firm to the bite), then drain. Toss the hot drained pasta with the hot spicy sauce, then with the cheese and serve immediately, with a spoonful of tapénade over each portion.

bayou gnocchi

111

fettucine with red and yellow pepper
purée and goat cheese

Serves 4 to 6

2 each: red and yellow bell
  peppers, roasted, peeled,
  and sliced
3 cloves garlic, chopped
5 Tbsp (65 mL) extra-virgin
  olive oil
1 egg, lightly beaten
1 lb (500 g) fresh fettucine
4 oz (125 g) mild soft goat
  cheese
5–6 Tbsp (65–80 mL) fresh basil,
  sliced
Salt and black pepper to taste

This is a sort of sweet pepper carbonara of tender roasted peppers puréed into a sauce with egg and olive oil, tossed with hot pasta until it cooks just enough to coat the noodles, then enriched with goat cheese and perfumed with a little basil. This is an impressive summer dish, which is very easy to prepare.

Preparation time: 20 minutes Cooking time: 5–10 minutes

Combine the peppers with the garlic, olive oil, and egg and purée until it forms a slightly chunky sauce.

Cook the fettucine until al dente (tender, but still firm to the bite), then drain. Return to the hot saucepan, add the pepper-egg sauce and toss quickly so that the egg cooks and coats the pasta rather than scrambling.

Remove from the heat and add the goat cheese, stirring as it melts, followed by the basil. Season to taste with salt and pepper and serve immediately while still very hot.

tagliatelle with *roasted peppers and cream*

Serves 4

5 to 7 cloves garlic, chopped
4 Tbsp (50 mL) butter
1 each: red, yellow, green bell
  pepper, roasted, peeled, and
  sliced
1 cup (200 mL) dry white wine
1½ cups (350 mL) heavy cream
Salt and black pepper to taste
1 lb (500 g) fresh tagliatelle
Freshly grated Parmesan cheese
  to taste

A white wine cream sauce, studded with sliced roasted peppers, and topped with some freshly grated Parmesan cheese — this is a simple but elegant and relatively inexpensive dish.

Preparation time: 15–20 minutes Cooking time: 15–20 minutes

Gently cook the garlic in the butter until it softens but does not fry or brown; add the peppers and cook for a few minutes.

Pour in the white wine, increase the heat, and cook until reduced to only a few tablespoons. Stir in the cream and lower the heat, allowing the cream to form a smooth sauce. Remove pan from the heat, season with salt and pepper, cover, and keep warm.

Cook the pasta in rapidly boiling salted water until al dente (tender, but still firm to the bite), then drain well.

Toss the hot pasta with the sauce, then serve immediately in shallow bowls or plates sprinkled generously with grated Parmesan.

orzo with roasted chiles, *chile-lime butter, and grated cheese*

Tender pasta, with a nip of hot chile and the

tang of lime, balanced with the richness of melted cheese.

Preparation time: 10–15 minutes Cooking time: 5–10 minutes

Serves 4

Cook the pasta in rapidly boiling salted water until just tender.

Meanwhile, mix the garlic with the chili powder, paprika, cumin, chopped chiles, chopped peppers, and olive oil, then stir in the butter, reserving 1 tablespoon, and mix well. Taste for seasoning and mix in the lime juice.

Drain the pasta, mix with the remaining butter and then with the cheese. Dust with black pepper and serve immediately, as a side dish or appetizer.

1½ cups (375 mL) orzo or other smallish shaped dried pasta
Salt to taste
7 cloves garlic, chopped
½–1 tsp (2–5 mL) mild chili powder and paprika, or to taste
¼–½ tsp (1–2 mL) cumin, or to taste
1 mild chile, such as poblano, roasted, peeled, and chopped
1 red bell pepper, roasted, peeled, and chopped
2 Tbsp (25 mL) olive oil
8 Tbsp (90 mL) butter, softened or at room temperature
Juice of ¼ lime, or to taste
1¼ cups (300 mL) Cheddar cheese, grated
Black pepper

macaroni and cheese *with chiles and chèvre*

Macaroni and cheese is a classic comfort food, especially when the weather is cold. This version includes goat cheese and mild chiles.

Serves 4

12 oz (350 g) macaroni

4 Tbsp (50 mL) butter

1 Tbsp (15 mL) all-purpose flour

1 cup (250 mL) milk

Salt and a few pinches cayenne pepper to taste

Grated nutmeg to taste

1 to 2 mild green chiles, roasted, peeled, and sliced

3–4 oz (100–125 g) chèvre or other mild goat cheese

Sour cream to taste (optional)

Several generous pinches thyme

2 to 3 cloves garlic, chopped

1 Tbsp (15 mL) paprika

10 oz (300 g) grated mild white cheese, such as mozzarella, Cheddar, fontina, or a combination

Preparation time: 20 minutes Cooking time: 25 minutes

Preheat the oven to 375°F (190°C).

Cook the pasta until al dente (tender, but still firm to the bite), then drain.

Heat the butter until foamy then sprinkle in the flour and cook for a few minutes. Remove from the heat and whisk in the milk. Cook, whisking, until the sauce thickens.

Combine the pasta with the sauce, season with salt, cayenne pepper, and nutmeg, then add the shredded green chile and the goat cheese, a few tablespoons of sour cream to taste, if using, thyme, garlic, paprika, and two-thirds of the cheese.

Arrange in a baking pan and top with the remaining cheese.

Bake until lightly browned, and the macaroni hot and sizzling, about 20 minutes. You could garnish with some roasted chiles and a dusting of paprika if liked. Serve immediately.

sandwiches
& pastries

Roasted peppers are a fundamental part of my sandwich repertoire and make an excellent topping for crostini or bruschetta. Indeed, many of the salads and appetizers in the various chapters can be eaten as crostini and bruschetta by serving them on a piece of toasted country bread.

milanese melted cheese
and pepper sandwiches

In Milan, toasted cheese sandwiches are made like this: the cheese is laid over the bread then topped with either olives, roasted peppers, or pickled vegetables and peppers, and so on. The sandwich is then closed, pressed tightly, and browned.

Serves 4

8 large slices bread, sliced thin

2½–3½ cups (600–900 mL) shredded white cheese, such as fontina, Cheddar, or Monterey Jack

3 cloves garlic, chopped

2 red bell peppers, roasted, peeled, and sliced (or bottled peppers can be used)

10 to 15 pimiento-stuffed green olives, sliced

2–3 Tbsp (25–45 mL) olive oil or 1 oz (25 g) butter

Preparation time: 5–10 minutes Cooking time: 5–10 minutes

Sprinkle 4 slices of the bread with half of the cheese, then with the garlic, peppers, and olives, finishing off with the rest of the cheese. Top with the second piece of bread and press together.

Heat the olive oil or butter in a skillet and gently brown the sandwiches, turning once or twice as the cheese melts and holds the bread together. Some of the cheese will ooze out and crisp up in the skillet, which is delicious, even if it burns slightly.

Serve hot, on a napkin-lined plate (either fabric or paper) to absorb the excess cooking fat.

mediterranean mixed pepper tart
with black olives and cheese

Crisp pie crust filled with a layer of tapénade, then lots of peppers stewed with tomatoes, topped with melted cheese. Serve this Mediterranean pepper tart as an appetizer or a tapaslike snack, with drinks.

Preparation time: 15 minutes Cooking time: 45 minutes

Preheat the oven to 400°F (200°C). Sauté the peppers in the olive oil until softened, about 5 minutes, then add the tomatoes and garlic and cook over medium-high heat until the mixture is thick, a further 5 to 8 minutes.

Remove from the heat, season with sugar. Allow to cool.

Roll out the dough and press it into a pie pan (9½-in/24-cm in diameter). Top with buttered baking parchment and baking weights. Bake for 5 to 8 minutes or until lightly browned at the edges. Remove the parchment and allow to cool.

Spread the tapénade or olives over the pie crust base. Top with the peppers, then sprinkle with oregano, then the feta followed by the grated white cheese.

Reduce oven temperature to 375°F (190°C). Bake for 15 to 20 minutes or until the cheese has melted. Serve hot or at cool room temperature.

Serves 4

1 each: red, green, yellow bell pepper, sliced thin
2 Tbsp (25 mL) extra-virgin olive oil
4 to 5 ripe tomatoes, diced
5 to 6 cloves garlic, chopped
Pinch sugar
5–6 oz (150–160 g) puff pastry dough
2 Tbsp (25 mL) tapénade or ½ cup (125 mL) black olives in oil, pitted and diced
Pinch oregano
3 oz (75 g) feta cheese, crumbled
5 oz (150 g) white cheese such as Cheddar, mozzarella, fontina, or Gruyère

quesadillas *with mild red chile paste*

Queso is Spanish for cheese. Quesadillas are toasted cheese and chile sandwiches made on a tortilla instead of bread. You can add anything you like to the melted cheese, such as cooked meat or mushrooms.

Preparation time: 15 minutes Cooking time: 5 minutes 👥

Purée the garlic and add the salt, chile powders, cumin, diced tomato, orange juice, and oregano.

Lay out the tortillas on one or more baking sheets and smear with a little of the puréed chile paste. Scatter the red and green pepper strips over the tortillas, and top with the cheese.

Broil until the cheese melts and sizzles. Serve immediately, garnished with cilantro.

Serves 4

3 cloves garlic, chopped
Salt
1 Tbsp (15 mL) ground New Mexico chile powder
1 Tbsp (15 mL) ancho chile powder
¼ tsp (1 mL) cumin
1 ripe tomato, diced
Juice of ¼ orange
¼ tsp (1 mL) oregano, or to taste
8 corn or flour tortillas
1 each: red bell pepper and mild green chile or pepper, roasted, peeled, and sliced
2½–3 cups (300–350 g) shredded white cheese
1 Tbsp (15 mL) fresh chopped cilantro

tramezzini of chicken *with red pepper aïoli* *and basil*

Serves 4

8 small, thin slices good bread,
   preferably a good whole
   wheat granary bread or a
   firm-textured white
1 quantity Red Pepper Aïoli
   (p. 136)
1 small roasted chicken
   (approx. ³/₄ lb/350 g in
   weight), the meat taken off
   the bone and shredded
Handful fresh basil leaves

I first tasted these tramezzini in a café in Genoa.

Serve them with apéritifs before dinner.

Preparation time: 15 minutes

Spread the bread generously with the red pepper aïoli, then arrange the shredded chicken on 4 of the slices. Top with basil leaves and a second piece of the aïoli-spread bread and press together. Chill, covered with a slightly damp cloth, until ready to serve (no longer than an hour or so).

pastries filled with roasted peppers, *ricotta cheese, and basil*

Makes 6

10 oz (300 g) puff pastry
   dough
¹/₃–¹/₂ cup (65–125 mL) pesto or
   fresh chopped basil leaves
1 cup (250 mL) mozzarella or
   fontina, or a similar white,
   melting cheese, diced
2 red bell peppers, roasted,
   peeled, and diced (bottled
   is fine)
1 to 2 ripe tomatoes, diced
4–5 oz (125–150 g) ricotta
   cheese
2 to 3 cloves garlic, chopped

Light, crisp pastries fragrant with basil, bound together with creamy ricotta

cheese, melting mozzarella, and pieces of roasted pepper and tomato.

Preparation time: 20 minutes Cooking time: 15–20 minutes

Divide the dough into 6 equal pieces, then roll them into round flat disks. Place on baking sheet.

Spread half of each pastry with pesto, or sprinkle with basil leaves, leaving a border around the edge for sealing the pastries.

Mix the remaining ingredients together in a bowl and place a spoonful or two of this mixture on top of the pesto-spread dough or basil leaves. (Any leftover cheese mixture is delicious for stuffing chicken breasts or for spreading on bread to make a toasted cheese sandwich.)

Preheat the oven to 400°F (200°C).

Fold the pastry over, wetting the edges with a little water then seal tightly, pressing the edges together.

Bake for 15 to 20 minutes or until golden brown. Serve hot.

indian *garbanzo crêpe*

Sliced chiles and sweet green peppers give this garbanzo crêpe an Indian flavor.

Preparation time: 10–15 minutes Cooking time: 10–15 minutes

Pour the besan into a bowl and add the water little by little so that you work out the lumps as you are mixing it. It should be the consistency of a thick batter. Season with salt and pepper. Mix together the cumin, sliced chile, green pepper, garlic, and cilantro.

Preheat the broiler. Heat 2 or so tablespoons of vegetable oil in a wide, shallow skillet. When it is smoking, ladle in about one-sixth to a quarter of the batter, swirl it around, and sprinkle with the seasoning mixture.

Cook over medium-high heat until the bottom is browned, then place under the broiler and broil until the top cooks, sizzles, and lightly browns.

Serve immediately, cut into wedges.

Serves 4

4 cups (1 L) besan (garbanzo flour)
2¼ cups (500 mL) cold water
Salt and black pepper
Pinch cumin
1 hot green or red chile, chopped or sliced thin
1 green bell pepper, chopped fine
4 to 6 cloves garlic, chopped
⅓–½ cup (50–65 mL) fresh chopped cilantro
½ cup (100 mL) vegetable oil, or as needed

roasted green pepper *or chile,*
and cheese "pizzette"

Using naan bread or focaccia as the base for pizza is a useful short-cut. I quite often add green olives to this pizza, and red peppers instead of the green ones.

Makes 4

4 pieces naan bread or focaccia

2 green bell peppers, roasted, peeled, shredded, and tossed with cayenne pepper to taste, or 2 large mild green chiles, roasted, peeled, and shredded but not tossed with cayenne pepper (they will be spicy enough)

2 to 3 cloves garlic, chopped

4 oz (100 g) mild goat cheese, crumbled

¼–½ tsp (1–2 mL) thyme

4 oz (125 g) mozzarella cheese, shredded

3–4 Tbsp (45–50 mL) Parmesan or pecorino cheese, grated

2 Tbsp (25 mL) extra-virgin olive oil

Preparation time: 5–10 minutes Cooking time: 5–10 minutes

Preheat oven to 400°F (200°C).

Place the naan bread or focaccia pieces on a baking sheet and arrange the sliced peppers or chiles over this, then sprinkle with the garlic, crumbled goat cheese, thyme, mozzarella, and Parmesan or pecorino cheese, then drizzle with the olive oil.

Bake until the cheese has melted and is sizzling. Serve immediately.

cuban green *pepper hamburguesas*

Cuban sandwiches are robust and hearty. They differ

from other sandwiches in that they are pressed and flattened

while being heated in a heavy skillet.

Preparation time: 15 minutes Cooking time: 15 minutes

Combine the ground beef with the onion, pepper, garlic, and soy sauce. Form 4 long oblong patties roughly the same size as the bread rolls. Season with salt and pepper.

Heat the olive oil in a heavy skillet and add the patties; brown over medium-high heat, turning once or twice, until they are just cooked through (no longer pink).

Place the rolls, cut side down, in the hot skillet and lightly toast them, then turn them cut side up and place some sliced cheese on half of them, followed by a hot meat patty on top, and press tightly to seal. Place a heavy lid on the skillet, which will act like a weight and press the sandwiches down, slightly flattening them and melting the fillings into them.

Remove from the heat and spread the uncovered bread roll halves with the sauce or salsa of your choice, the pickled peppers, and a handful of salad leaves. Close the sandwiches up tightly and serve.

Serves 4

1 lb (500 g) lean ground beef
1 onion, chopped
1 green bell pepper, chopped
5 cloves garlic, chopped
1 Tbsp (15 mL) soy sauce
Salt and pepper to taste
2 Tbsp (25 mL) extra-virgin
   olive oil
4 soft oblong bread rolls, split
   lengthwise in half
4–5 oz (100–150 g) cheese,
   such as Cheddar, mozzarella,
   or Provolone, sliced thin
Red Pepper Aïoli (p. 136) or
   mayonnaise and Provençal
   Red Pepper Mustard (p. 134)
   or tomato salsa, as desired
Sweet pickled peppers
Handful salad leaves, lightly
   dressed in olive oil and
   balsamic vinegar

roasted pepper, *salami, and ham pie*

Serves 4 to 6

3 red or yellow bell peppers
5 cloves garlic, chopped
1–2 tsp (5–10 mL) red wine
   vinegar
Salt and pepper
5 Tbsp (65 mL) extra-virgin
   olive oil
1¾ lb (750 g) spinach
10 oz (300 g) short pastry
   dough
7 oz (200 g) Cheddar or
   fontina cheese, sliced thin
3½ oz (100 g) salami or chorizo
   sausage, sliced thin
3½ oz (100 g) ham,
   sliced thin

Pastry filled with marinated peppers, cheese, ham, and salami,

this is a classic picnic dish found in many parts of Italy.

Preparation time: 30 minutes Cooking time: 20–25 minutes

Roast the peppers until evenly charred, then peel and cut into large slices. Toss the roasted peppers with half the garlic, vinegar, salt and pepper, and half the olive oil. Set aside.

Heat the remaining garlic in the remaining olive oil until just fragrant, then add the spinach and cook for a few moments in the garlicky oil. Season with salt and pepper and allow to cool.

Preheat the oven to 400°F (200°C).

Roll out half of the dough and place it onto a lightly floured work surface. Arrange a bottom layer of one-third of the cheese, all the spinach, half the salami, and half the ham, then top with a further third of the cheese, all the peppers, the remaining half of the salami followed by the remaining half of the ham, and finish with the remaining cheese.

Top with the second half of the rolled out pastry, wet the edges, and pinch together to seal.

Make slits in the top of the pie crust with a sharp knife, to allow the steam to escape, and bake for 20 to 35 minutes or until golden brown. Serve hot, warm, or at room temperature.

red pepper *torta*

Serves 4 to 6

4 red bell peppers, roasted,
   peeled, and chopped
4 Tbsp (50 mL) butter,
   preferably unsalted
1½ lb (750 g) ricotta cheese
Salt and pepper to taste
3½ oz (85 g) Parmesan cheese,
   freshly grated
1 tsp (5 mL) thyme or fresh
   rosemary, crushed
2 eggs, lightly beaten
1½–2 cups (375–500 mL) fine
   bread crumbs

This torta of roasted red peppers mixed with creamy ricotta cheese,

baked in a crisp crumb crust, tastes even better the next day.

Preparation time: 15–20 minutes Cooking time: 40 minutes

Preheat oven to 325°F (160°C).

Lightly sauté the red peppers in half the butter. Remove from the heat, then mix in the ricotta, salt and pepper, Parmesan, thyme or rosemary, and eggs.

Rub the inside of a 1-quart (1-l) soufflé dish with the remaining butter, then sprinkle the inside with the crumbs, turning the dish to coat the insides evenly.

Gently spoon in the red pepper and cheese mixture. Bake the torta for about 40 minutes or until firm and puffed up. Serve hot or cold.

roasted pepper, salami, and ham pie

roasted red pepper *pita bread*

Roasted red pepper, kneaded into the dough, gives this flatbread an unusual

flavor. Homemade pita bread tastes good made on the barbecue.

Makes about 6

2 tsp (10 mL) dried yeast

Pinch sugar

²/₃ cup (150 mL) warm water, or
   as needed

1 lb (500 g) unbleached white
   flour

1 Tbsp (15 mL) fresh thyme

1 tsp (5 mL) salt

1 Tbsp (15 mL) extra-virgin
   olive oil, plus a little extra

2 red bell peppers, roasted,
   peeled, and chopped

Preparation time: 20 minutes Proving time: 1¹/₂ hours Cooking time: 8–10 minutes

Dissolve the yeast with the sugar in about ¹/₃ cup of warm water and leave for about 10 minutes or until frothy. If it fails to froth, start again (your yeast may be old or the temperature of the room may be too cool).

In a large bowl, mix the flour with the thyme, salt, and oil, then add the yeast, remaining water, and red peppers and begin mixing with a fork. When it gets too hard to mix with a fork, start kneading with your hands on a floured board. Knead for about 10 minutes or until smooth and elastic.

Pour the olive oil into a large bowl and swirl it around to coat the sides. Place the dough in this bowl, cover with plastic wrap and leave in a warm place for about an hour and a half, or until doubled in size.

Punch the dough down, and divide it into 6 equal pieces. Roll out each piece on a lightly floured board with a floured rolling pin until about 8 in (20 cm) in diameter and about ¹/₄ in (5 mm) thick.

Arrange them on a floured surface such as a board or plates and leave for about 30 minutes or until they have risen slightly and are puffy.

Preheat the oven to 425˚F (220˚C).

Transfer the pitas to ungreased nonstick baking sheets and bake for 8 to 10 minutes or until puffed up and lightly golden. It is better to underbake rather than overbake pitas.

Helpful hint

Any unbaked dough can be frozen, tightly wrapped, for up to 6 months and defrosted before baking.

accompaniments

Peppers make the perfect accompaniment to anything except dessert. They can enhance any kebob or salad. Broiled peppers and chiles are marvelous accompaniments for a wide variety of barbecued foods across the world, from Marakkech to Mexico City, Bangkok to Bulgaria, Tuscany to Thailand.

whole broiled peppers
to accompany any barbecue

Whether you find yourself in North Africa, Turkey, or the streets of Mexico, a barbecue will invariably include peppers. They should be lightly grilled — not charred black as you would with peppers you are going to peel — then stemmed, seeded, and eaten, skin and all.

Preparation time: 5 minutes Cooking time: 5–10 minutes

In Mexico, you'll find incendiary little jalapeños grilled over an open fire with scallions alongside. Serve them with barbecued meat or spiced fish tacos. In Turkey a selection of green, light yellow-green, and nearly-yellow twisting peppers are cooked on the barbecue with lamb kebobs. In North Africa, large mild green or red chiles are grilled and served around a platter of couscous, as a garnish to accompany other colorful vegetables. Large grilled, whole mild chiles are often served in falafel stands as part of the salad selections, especially in Tel Aviv. Try one inside your falafel and salad pita.

A few grilled mild and hot chiles, cooked on the barbecue, go well with any ground meat and herb kebobs. Serve with salad, hummus, and warm pita bread.

fiery little *devils*

Makes 8

8 jalapeño chiles, either all
   green or a combination
   of green and red
1 batch fresh salsa of your
   choice

These are extremely spicy, so don't try them without working your way up: start just nibbling at their tip until you get used to the fire. They pack quite a punch.

Preparation time: 10–15 minutes 🌶🌶🌶🌶 **(VERY HOT – BEWARE)**

Working one by one lay a chile on its side and cut a little slice from one side, essentially forming a boatlike container. Scoop out the seeds and discard; reserve the piece of chile you have cut off for making salsa.

Using a small pointed spoon, fill each hollowed-out chile boat with salsa.

Arrange the chiles on a plate and serve with caution!

whole broiled peppers

127

turkish hot pepper *and tomato salsa*

Serves 4

1½ lb (750 g) ripe red
    tomatoes, diced, or 14-oz
    (398-mL) can chopped
    tomatoes
Salt to taste
Small pinch sugar
1 small to medium-sized onion,
    chopped fine
1 to 3 medium to medium-hot
    fresh red chiles
1–2 Tbsp (15–25 mL) extra-
    virgin olive oil
3 cloves garlic, chopped
Juice and zest of ½ to 1 lemon
½–⅔ cup (65–80 mL) fresh
    chopped parsley or cilantro

This lively sauce is spicy without being frighteningly hot.

If you prefer more fire, simply increase the amount of hot pepper to taste.

Preparation time: 10–15 minutes Cooking time: 10–15 minutes

Place the tomatoes in a small nonstick saucepan and cook over medium heat, stirring occasionally with a wooden spoon, until the tomatoes cook down and reduce in volume to about 3 to 4 tablespoons. Season with salt and sugar and allow to cool.

Combine with the onion, chiles, olive oil, garlic, lemon juice, lemon zest, and parsley or cilantro. Chill until ready to serve.

Helpful hint

Enjoy with broiled or barbecued meat or fish, or with eggs, rice pilaf, or simply spread on bread. A spoonful added to salad dressing gives it a piquant flavor.

sue kreitzman's roasted *red pepper sauce*

Makes about 1½ cups (350 ml)

3 red bell peppers, roasted,
    peeled, and chopped
2 to 3 cloves garlic, chopped
Hot sauce or tabasco
¼ tsp (1 mL) cumin, or to taste

Inspired by European food writer Sue Kreitzman,

this simply made, highly flavorsome sauce contains no fat.

Use as a sauce, dip, salad dressing, or sandwich filling.

Preparation time: 5–10 minutes

Purée the roasted, peeled red peppers in a food processor, then add the remaining ingredients. Process until it forms a smooth purée. Chill until ready to serve.

Helpful hint

The quantity given here is enough to serve as a dip for crudités, or to cover 3 to 4 portions of fish, chicken breast, or other meat.

chinese red pepper dipping sauce
with soy, ginger, and cilantro

Delicious with a selection of dim sum, this quick dipping sauce can be easily and successfully made with bottled peppers.

Preparation time: 5–10 minutes

Combine all the ingredients except the cilantro in a blender and process until smooth. Chill until ready to use. Serve sprinkled with cilantro.

Serves 4

5 oz (150 g) red peppers, roasted, peeled, and diced (about 2 bottled peppers)

2 cloves garlic, chopped

1–2 tsp (5–10 mL) each: sesame oil, soy sauce, and vinegar

½ tsp (2 mL) sugar

¼ tsp (1 mL) hot pepper flakes or cayenne pepper

1 tsp (5 mL) ginger root, chopped fine

5–6 Tbsp (65–75 mL) fresh chopped cilantro

israeli pepper *relish*

This relish, or salad appetizer, known as *Horef*, is made with mixed sweet

and hot peppers, tomatoes, and spices.

Serves 4

2 green bell peppers, cut into
thick slices
2 mild green chiles, sliced
2 to 3 medium-hot green
chiles, sliced
5 to 7 cloves garlic, chopped
5 Tbsp (65 mL) extra-virgin
olive oil
1–1¼ lb (500–600 g) fresh
tomatoes, diced, or 14-oz
(398-mL) can chopped
tomatoes
1 tsp (5 mL) curry powder
Seeds from 2 to 3 cardamom
pods or a pinch of ground
cardamom
Pinch each: cumin, turmeric,
and dried ginger
Pinch sugar to taste
Salt and pepper to taste
Juice of ½ lemon, or to taste

Preparation time: 10 minutes Cooking time: 10 minutes

Lightly sauté the peppers, chiles, and garlic in the olive oil until softened, then add
the tomatoes, curry powder, and other spices and continue to cook until you have a
rich, thickened mixture.

Season to taste with sugar and salt and pepper, and add lemon juice to taste.
Chill until ready to serve.

Helpful hint

Serve with pita bread and falafel, or as an accompaniment to barbecued meat or
fish. It also goes well with plain boiled chicken.

accompaniments

hot pepper *and lime paste*

This hot flavorful paste, based on the Sudanese dish *shaata*, is made with mild chiles, paprika, and freshly squeezed lime juice. Increase the quantity as required by simply doubling or trebling the recipe.

Preparation time: 5 minutes Standing time: 10+ minutes

Stir all the ingredients together and mix well. Allow to stand for at least 10 minutes before serving, so the flavors can develop.

Helpful hint
The paste is delicious added to stews, spicy soups, or Asian noodle dishes. It can also be a marinade for barbecued foods. Spread it sparingly over bread and top with cheese, meat, or fish for a zesty sandwich.

Makes about 2 Tbsp (25 mL)

1 Tbsp (15 mL) mild chili powder or ancho chile powder
1–2 tsp (5–10 mL) paprika
Juice of ½ lime, more if needed
Several generous pinches of salt

coulis de poivrons *rouges aux tomates*

Easy to prepare, this French raw red pepper and tomato sauce makes a lively accompaniment to a number of dishes and is a delicious basis for soufflés, soups, or vinaigrette dressing. It can also be added to other, complementary sauces to brighten up their flavor, and freezes well.

Preparation time: 15 minutes Cooking time: 15–20 minutes

In a heavy saucepan lightly sauté the onion in the olive oil until softened, then add the garlic and red peppers and continue to cook until they are softened as well.

Add the tomatoes, cover, and cook until the mixture is saucelike, then add the tomato juice or tomato paste and water and bring to a boil. Cook for about 5 minutes or until the mixture is quite soft, stirring continuously.

Allow to cool, then purée in a blender or food processor. Season to taste with salt, pepper, cayenne or tabasco, sugar, and herbs.

Makes about 1½ cups (350 mL)

1 onion, chopped
1 Tbsp (15 mL) extra-virgin olive oil
3 to 4 cloves garlic, chopped
2 red bell peppers, chopped
2 fresh or canned tomatoes, diced
¼ cup (60 mL) tomato juice or 1 Tbsp (15 mL) tomato paste mixed with ¼ cup (60 mL) water (optional)
Salt and pepper
Pinch cayenne pepper or tabasco to taste
Pinch sugar to taste
Large pinch herbs as desired: thyme, marjoram, herbes de Provence, etc.

salsa *verde*

Makes about 2¹/₂-3 cups (600-750 mL)

2 lb (1 kg) fresh tomatillos or 2 medium-sized cans tomatillos (green tomatoes)

¹/₂ onion, chopped

Salt to taste

1 poblano, Anaheim, or other mild green chile, chopped (use a green bell pepper if you want a milder salsa)

1 to 2 fresh hot or medium-hot chiles, such as jalapeños, chopped (or less if you want a milder salsa)

2 to 3 cloves garlic, chopped

¹/₄-¹/₂ tsp (1-2 mL) cumin, or to taste (optional)

3 to 4 Tbsp (45-50 mL) fresh chopped cilantro

Salsa Verde is made with chiles and tomatillos, small green husk tomatoes with a delightfully fresh, sour flavor. This salsa goes well with any taco.

Preparation time: 15 minutes Cooking time: 10 minutes

If using fresh tomatillos remove their brown papery husks. Underneath the husks the skin of the tomatillos will be sticky. Rinse them, but do not worry about rinsing off all of the stickiness: it will not come off, but will dissolve during cooking.

Cut the tomatillos in half and place in a saucepan with a few tablespoons of water. Cover and bring to a boil over medium heat; cook for 5 to 10 minutes, adding more water if wished, until the tomatillos are very tender and soft.

Remove from the heat and allow to cool slightly. (You can prepare this salsa with hot tomatillos, too, and the result will be delicious though slightly different, as the onion, chile, and other ingredients will cook very slightly with the heat of the tomatillos.)

Purée the tomatillos in a blender or food processor or mash by hand. Add the onion, salt, chopped chile, garlic, cumin, and cilantro. Use immediately, or chill until ready to use, preferably within the day.

salsa *cruda*

Serves 4 to 6

3 to 5 jalapeño chiles, chopped

1 mild green chile, such as poblano or Anaheim, chopped (optional)

3 scallions, chopped fine

5 cloves garlic, chopped

3 to 5 ripe flavorful tomatoes, diced (include a little tomato juice or sauce to boost the tomato flavor, if wished)

Pinch sugar

¹/₄ tsp (1 mL) cumin, or more to taste

Salt to taste

5-6 Tbsp (65-75 mL) fresh chopped cilantro

Juice of ¹/₂ lemon or lime

This classic, chunky mixture of chiles and a few flavorings defines Mexican cuisine around the world and is very healthful as well.

Preparation time: 15 minutes

Combine the chiles with the scallions, garlic, and tomatoes, then season with the sugar, cumin, and salt.

Toss with the cilantro and lemon or lime juice and taste for seasoning. Serve immediately or chill until ready to serve, preferably within the day.

salsa cruda

133

provençal red *pepper mustard*

Red pepper mustard adds a certain Mediterranean and Louisiana Creole flavor to plain French mustard. The quantity given here is enough for several sandwiches, or to add to one or two large bowls of salad.

Makes about 4–5 Tbsp (50–65 mL)

1 Tbsp (15 mL) each: mild French light-brown mustard and Dijon mustard
½ red bell pepper, roasted, peeled, and chopped fine
1 tsp (5 mL) paprika
½ clove garlic, chopped, or more to taste
¼ tsp (1 mL) balsamic vinegar, or more to taste
Several dashes hot sauce
Several pinches herbes de Provence

Preparation time: 5 minutes

Mix all the ingredients together and taste for seasoning. You could sprinkle with a little more paprika if liked.

roasted onion *and chile salsa*

Roasting brings out a different side of the chile, as well as the onions and garlic. Roasting mellows the harshness and draws out the sweetness, giving this salsa a completely different character to those that are raw or simmered.

Preparation time: 10 minutes Cooking time: 10–15 minutes

In a heavy ungreased skillet place the onion, garlic, chiles, and green pepper and heat until they char on one side then turn them to char the other side. Cover with a lid and allow to cool, covered, steaming in their own juices.

When cool enough to handle, remove their skins and stems (remove the seeds from the chiles), and chop. Combine ingredients in a bowl. Season with salt and lemon juice to taste.

Serves 4 to 6

1 onion, unpeeled, cut in half
10 cloves garlic, whole and
  unpeeled
3 medium-hot chiles such as
  jalapeño or Kenya, whole
1 green bell pepper, cut
  in half
Salt to taste
Juice of ½ to 1 lemon,
  or to taste

accompaniments

135

red pepper *aïoli*

Serves 4

6 Tbsp (75 mL) mayonnaise
2 cloves garlic, chopped
⅛–¼ tsp (0.5–1 mL) cumin, or
  to taste
½ tsp (2 mL) each: mild red
  chili powder and paprika, or
  more to taste
Salt and pepper to taste
1–2 Tbsp (15–25 mL) extra-
  virgin olive oil
Juice of ¼ to ½ lemon
½ red bell pepper, chopped fine

Red pepper, sweet, flavorful, and slightly crunchy, dots this delightfully spicy aïoli. The mild chili powder flavors the mayonnaise without adding too much fire. Delicious on sandwiches, especially one made with leftover *Vaca Frita* (p. 79) or barbecued pork, fish fillet, or chicken.

Preparation time: 5–10 minutes

Combine the mayonnaise with the garlic, cumin, chili powder, paprika, and salt and pepper. Gradually whisk in the olive oil until it emulsifies, then add the lemon juice. Finally, stir in the chopped pepper. Chill until ready to serve.

pickled green chiles

*Makes ½–1 pint
(230–470 mL)*

1 to 2 onions, peeled and sliced
  thick
10 cloves garlic, cut lengthwise
  into half
3 carrots, sliced thin
2 to 10 jalapeños, whole,
  halved, or sliced
2 Tbsp (25 mL) olive oil
Salt to taste
Mixture of half vinegar and
  half water, to cover
¼–½ tsp (1–2 mL) fresh
  crushed oregano leaves, or to
  taste
¼–½ tsp (1–2 mL) cumin,
  either toasted seeds or
  ground powder, or to taste
Black pepper to taste

This pickle is known in Mexico as *Jalapeños en Escabeche*. The quantity and type of chile will influence the heat of this pickle, so too will how you prepare it: whole chiles make a milder pickle; sliced, the chile fires up the entire mixture.

Preparation time: 10–15 minutes Cooking time: 5 minutes

Lightly sauté the onions, garlic, carrots, and jalapeños in the oil until slightly softened and limp, then add the salt, vinegar, water, oregano, cumin, and black pepper.

Bring to a boil and cook over high heat for about 10 minutes. The vegetables should be lightly cooked but still crisp.

Allow to cool, and eat as desired. To keep as fresh, store covered in a sterilized jar or bowl in the refrigerator for a maximum of 2 weeks.

If you want to store it for a longer period, proceed as for any sealed preserve or pickle, using enough salt and sterile jars or bottles, as well as observing other safety procedures (p. 18).

mango *and red pepper salsa*

This mild salsa can double as a salad: just decrease the quantity of chiles. It can be made spicier by increasing the quantity of chiles, or adding a dash or two of hot sauce.

Preparation time: 10–15 minutes

Combine the mango with the red pepper, chiles, garlic, lime, sugar, red onion, and cilantro, and a pinch of salt if needed.

Chill until ready to serve.

Helpful hint

This salsa is particularly good with chile-marinated chicken breast or seafood.

Serves 4

2 ripe mangos, peeled and diced
1 red bell pepper, diced
$^1/_2$ red chile, chopped
$^1/_2$ green chile, chopped
2 cloves garlic, chopped
Juice of 1 lime
1 tsp (5 mL) sugar, or to taste
$^1/_4$ to $^1/_2$ red onion, chopped
6–7 Tbsp (75–80 mL) fresh chopped cilantro
Pinch salt to taste, if needed

jellies

Red Chile Jelly (Mild)

5 mild red chiles, chopped
(more if wished or if your
chiles are very very mild)

2 red bell peppers, chopped

1½ cups (350 mL) cider vinegar
or white wine vinegar

3 cups (750 mL) sugar

⅔ cup (150 mL) liquid pectin or
2–2½ oz (50–60 g) powdered
pectin

Few drops red food coloring
(optional)

Yellow Pepper Jelly with Jalapeños (Medium)

6 jalapeño chiles, preferably
red, or a combination of
jalapeño and wax peppers for
a milder jelly

2 yellow bell peppers, chopped

1½ cups (350 mL) cider vinegar
or white wine vinegar

3 cups (750 mL) sugar

⅔ cup (150 mL) liquid pectin or
2–2½ oz (50–60 g) powdered
pectin

Few drops yellow food coloring
(optional)

Green Chile Jelly with Poblanos (Hot)

3 mild chiles, such as poblanos
or Anaheims

4 to 6 fresh hot green chiles,
such as jalapeños, chopped

2 green bell peppers, chopped

1½ cups (350 mL) cider vinegar
or white wine vinegar

3 cups (750 mL) sugar

⅔ cup (150 mL) liquid pectin or
2–2½ oz (50–60 g) powdered
pectin

Few drops green food coloring
(optional)

The heat of hot pepper jelly depends on the type of hot pepper used. You can add a drop or two of food coloring to boost the color of a particularly pale mixture. Serve as a glaze for rich meats such as duck or lamb, or as a chutneylike accompaniment to ham or cold turkey.

Preparation time: 45–60 minutes Cooking time: 2 minutes

Combine the chiles, peppers, vinegar, and sugar and purée. Bring to a boil, stirring, then remove from the heat and add the pectin.

Return to the heat and boil for 2 minutes, or follow the directions on the pectin package if they differ. Remove surface scum, stir, and leave to settle for 5 minutes. Remove any white scum and pour into sterilized jars (p. 18), leaving a little space (¼ in/5 mm) at the top and seal.

ancho chile *and sweet pepper preserves*

This sweet-spicy condiment is appreciated by even timid palates. The sweet flavor delicately balances the spicy heat, and allows the rich ancho chile flavor to emerge. Serve with barbecued burgers or as a condiment to chicken stew or roasted duck.

Preparation time: 15 minutes Cooking time: 15–20 minutes

Combine the peppers and chiles then add the remaining ingredients. Bring to a boil, then reduce the heat and simmer, adding more water if the mixture appears to be in danger of burning (it will caramelize, thicken, and reduce); this should take about 10 to 15 minutes. Watch it carefully, because it could burn easily.

Allow to cool, pour into a little pot, and cover. Refrigerate until ready to serve. This will keep for up to two weeks, covered, in the refrigerator. For a longer-lasting preserve, spoon into sterilized jars and seal either by sealing wax or using lids and boiling in a pan of water (p. 18).

Makes about 1–1 1/2 cups (250–350 mL)

2 red bell peppers, or 1 red and 1 orange bell pepper, diced
2 tsp (10 mL) ground ancho chiles or 2 whole ancho chile pods, lightly roasted over an open flame, then sliced thin with scissors
1/2–1 tsp (2–5 mL) paprika
1/2 cup (90 mL) cider vinegar or white wine vinegar
3–5 Tbsp (45–60 mL) water
Pinch cinnamon
1/3 cup (50 mL) light brown sugar, or to taste

zucchini *and pepper chutney*

This chutney recipe was inspired by a trip through the vegetable wonderland of New Spitalfields Market in London, England.

Preparation time: 15–20 minutes
Cooking time: 15–20 minutes Standing time: 3 hours

Combine the sliced zucchini, onions, peppers, chile, and garlic with the salt. Cover with coarsely broken ice cubes and mix thoroughly. Allow to stand for 3 hours then drain but do not rinse.

Combine the remaining ingredients with the vegetable mixture in a heavy pot and heat to boiling point. Remove from the heat and seal in hot sterilized jars (p. 18). Refrigerate once opened.

Makes 8–10 pints (3.5–4.5 L)

4 1/2 lb (2 kg) zucchini, cut lengthwise in half then sliced about 1/4–1/2 in thick
6 onions, sliced lengthwise
1 each: red, green, yellow bell pepper, diced
1 mild red chile, chopped
6 cloves garlic, sliced
1/2 cup (75 mL) coarse salt
ice cubes
3 cups (750 mL) sugar
1 cup (250 mL) seedless raisins
1 Tbsp (15 mL) turmeric
1 Tbsp (15 mL) celery seeds
2 Tbsp (25 mL) mustard seeds
5 Tbsp (65 mL) chopped ginger root
2 Tbsp (25 mL) whole-seed mustard
3 cups (750 mL) cider vinegar

pineapple and *roasted red pepper salsa*

Serves 4

½ ripe sweet pineapple, peeled,
  cored, and diced
½ red onion, chopped fine
1 red bell pepper, roasted,
  peeled, and diced
½ habanero or Scotch bonnet,
  or habanero-type chile such
  as the slightly milder rocoto,
  chopped (optional)
2 cloves garlic, chopped
Juice of ½ lime, or to taste
Zest of ¼ to ½ lime, or to taste
Sugar to taste

Pineapple brings out the sweet fruity flavor of the red pepper. I like to make it

using roasted red peppers but it is equally good, though slightly different,

made with fresh raw peppers. Serve with rich, spicy barbecued pork or duck.

If liked you can add half a habanero or rocoto chile to give it heat.

Preparation time: 15 minutes

Combine all the ingredients and chill until ready to serve.

mixed melon *and red chile relish*

This is a refreshing accompaniment to cold roasted chicken and a

grain salad such as *tabbouleh*, with a fresh green salad on the side.

Preparation time: 10–15 minutes 🌶🌶🌶🌶

Combine all the ingredients and chill until ready to serve.

About ¼ small-sized
watermelon (about 2 to 3
portions), rind removed, cut
into small pieces, seeded if
necessary
¼ to ½ ripe but firm green-
fleshed melon, such as Ogen,
Galia, or honeydew, rind and
seeds removed, cut into small
pieces
¼ orange-fleshed melon, such
as Charentais or Cantaloupe,
rind and seeds removed, cut
into small pieces
1 medium-hot fresh red chile,
such as jalapeño or serrano,
or to taste, sliced thin or
chopped
Juice of ½ lime
¼ red onion, sliced very thin
Salt to taste
Sugar to taste

thai mango, papaya, *and chile relish*

Serves 4

2 underripe green mangos,
  peeled and sliced thin
1 underripe green papaya,
  peeled and sliced thin
2 to 3 dry-fleshed chiles such
  as cayenne or Thai red and
  green chiles, sliced thin
  crosswise
Sugar to taste
Salt to taste

Serve this relish as a side dish with rich barbecued foods,

rice, and curries. The mango and papaya must be underripe.

Preparation time: 10–15 minutes 🌶🌶🌶🌶🌶

Serve the sliced mango and papaya sprinkled with half the chiles and allow each diner
to sprinkle on salt and sugar and more sliced chiles if they wish, all to taste.

accompaniments

Index

Useful Addresses

The Cook's Garden
PO Box 5010
Hodges, SC 29653-5010
Toll-Free 1-800-457-9703
Fax Toll-Free 1-800-457-9705
http://www.cooksgarden.com
Features choice selection of hot and sweet peppers, including the Boldog Paprika, Purple Beauty, Chocolate Beauty and Corno di Toro, a mix of red and yellow Bull's Horn peppers from Italy.

The Gourmet Gardener
8650 College Blvd, Suite 205IN
Overland Park, KS 66210-1806
(913) 345-0490
http://www.gourmetgardener.com
Limited but specialized choice of peppers, many European varieties.

Park Seed Co., Inc.
1 Parkton Avenue
Greenwood, SC 29647-0001
Toll-Free 1-800-845-3369
Fax (864) 941-4206
http://www.parkseeds.com
Large U.S.-based seed house offers wide selection of peppers, including Sweet Rainbow Mix, hot peppers plus Tomatillo Toma Verde.

The Pepper Gal
Box 23006
Ft. Lauderdale, FL 23307-3006
(954) 537-5540
Fax (954) 566-2208
Over 260 varieties of sweet, hot and ornamental peppers. Catalogue US$1.

Plants of the Southwest
Agua Fria Road, Rt 6 Box 11A
Santa Fe, NM 87501

Toll-Free 1-800-788-7333
Fax (505) 438-8800
http://www.plantsofthesouthwest.com
Drought-tolerant native plants and seeds. Chile Seed Collection consists of 25-35 packets of their available chiles. Hot 5 Seed Collection features Habanero, Piquin, Anaheim"M", NuMex Centennial and Thai. Ristra Collection offers 5 colorful chiles for 'ristras', or menus: NuMex Eclipse, Sunrise and Sunset, Chimayo and De Arbol.

Redwood City Seed Company
PO Box 361
Redwood City, CA 94064
(650) 325-7333
http://www.ecoseeds.com
Alternative seed company established in 1971 offers open-pollinated, old-fashioned varieties for home gardens. Select seeds include sweet Cubanelle, Quadrato d'Asti and Giallo plus Thai, Chinese and Mexican hot peppers. Features many "bird peppers" (very small, hot peppers) and a selection of rare imported seeds that vary each season. On-line or free printed catalogue. Mail-order only.

Seeds of Change
PO Box 15700
Santa Fe, NM 87506
Toll-Free 1-888-762-7333
http://www.seedsofchange.com
Select choice of certified organic, open-pollinated heirloom and traditional varieties. Pepper selection includes Bolivian Rainbow, Relleno, Nardello Sweet, Red Heart and Corno Di Toro.

Seeds Unique
1125 Barboa Court
Belen, NM 87002
(505) 861-0146
http://www.seedsonline.com

Variety of peppers, including the Chimayo, which thrives (and gets hotter) in a cooler climate.

Shepherd Garden Seeds
30 Irene Street
Torrington, CT 06790-6658
(860) 482-3638
Fax (860) 482-0532
http://wwwshepherdseeds.com
Choice selection of more than 15 heirloom peppers. Free catalogue; ships to U.S. only.

Southern Exposure Seed Exchange
PO Box 170
Earlysville, VA 22936
(804) 973-4703
Fax (804) 973-8717
http://www.southernexposure.com
Over 500 varieties of open-pollinated, heirloom and traditional vegetables, including over 40 hot and sweet peppers. Catalogue $2 U.S. and Canada.

Terra Time & Tide Seeds
590 East 59th Street
Jacksonville, FL 32208-4824
(904) 764-0376
http://www.pepperhot.com
Variety of hot peppers from Africa, Bolivia, Costa Rica, Vietnam, Mexico, India, Brazil, Peru, Thailand, Chile, Korea, Jamaica, Belize, Florida, and more.

Tomato Growers Supply Company
PO Box 2237
Fort Myers, FL 33902
Toll-Free 1-888-478-7333
Fax Toll-Free 1-888-768-3476
http://www.tomatogrowers.com
Family-owned company since 1984, specializing in tomatoes and peppers, including 135 pepper varieties. Also sells 335 tomato and several tomatillo varieties.